50 Years of Alpinism

50 Years of Alpinism

by
RICCARDO CASSIN

translated by
RENATO SOTTILE

DIADEM BOOKS LTD LONDON
THE MOUNTAINEERS SEATTLE

Published simultaneously in Britain by Diadem Books Ltd.
and in the United States by The Mountaineers, Seattle

All trade enquiries U.K. and Commonwealth to
Cordee, 249 Knighton Church Road, Leicester, England

All trade enquiries in the USA and Canada to
The Mountaineers, Books, 715 Pike Street, Seattle,
Washington 98101

British Library Cataloguing in Publication Data:
Cassin, Riccardo
50 Years of Alpinism.
1. Mountaineering
I. Title
796.5′22′0924 GV200

ISBN 0-906371-65-1 (UK)

Library of Congress Catalog Card Number 81-84329
ISBN 0-89886-060-1 (US)

Printed and bound in Great Britain
at The Pitman Press, Bath

Contents

Part 4: Karakoram: Rebuff and Success

Part 5: Expeditions

Part 6: Epilogue

List of Plates

between pages 32 and 33

between pages 64 and 65

Note: Uncredited photos are from the Cassin collection

Maps and Diagrams in the Text

Introduction

"Riccardo, why don't you write a book about it all — all your climbing adventures, from the first ones in the Pre-Alps, through the Alps and Dolomites to your successful international expeditions?"

I had often been asked that and often thought of it, with no great enthusiasm, but while I was going home on a military flight from the 1975 Lhotse Expedition, after failing on the South Face, the question returned to nag me. The flight had put me in a contemplative mood but those remembered voices, once friendly, became more and more demanding, to the point of upsetting my peace of mind.

But why did I remember them at that moment? It seemed almost ironic that it was the moment at which, for the first time in my life as a climber, my will had been forced into submission. A feeling of profound rebellion choked me. Intense and complex sensations added up or cancelled each other out: thus the joy of seeing my old friends increased the satisfaction of returning home with all the men of the expedition in such good form after so many dangers and difficulties; the thought of returning to the monotony of everyday life made the memory of that repulsive route even more loathsome, while the comfort of having done everything possible partially mollified the bitterness of defeat.

Yet these sensations were momentary. Years of spending all of my free time in the mountains had not only forged my character, but opened my heart to deep pragmatic introspection, so that while so many successes on hard climbs had given me self confidence and a feeling of power and strength, the Lhotse failure, after so much preparation, made me know exactly where the limits of human capacity take over from sheer will-power.

Mountains had once again proven to be life's masters, stretching and teaching, but still winning.

Within this account of my long climbing career lie the experiences which are the life-blood of a great yet ever-fresh love affair with mountains and everything that is a part of them.

PART 1

Early Years

CHAPTER ONE

The Mountains Above Lecco

1929: Climbs in the Resogne and the Grignetta — Punta Cermenati and Guglia Angelina

Climbers, like sailors and poets, are born not made. You can even be brought up in a landlocked area but if the passion for the sea is latent in you, even if unrecognised, then the moment you reach a port it explodes irrepressibly. The same is true of the mountains; if you are born for them, sooner or later you will find yourself drawn towards them with an attraction that may be violent.

That was what happened to Fritz Kasparek, one of the group of four who made the first ascent of the North Face of the Eiger. Living in Vienna, he would never have become a serious climber; but a girl he liked persuaded him to make a Sunday outing to Pilsten, the local rock climbing area (which is to Vienna like the Grigna is to Lombardy). Once was enough: he was hooked.

It also happened to Emilio Comici, the poet of Dolomite climbing. Born in Trieste, he took up the challenge of speleology; but when, in the Julian Alps, he found himself face to face with the North Wall of Madre dei Comosci, his innate passion, which he had never felt before, exploded with such a force that it changed his life.

I have compared climbers and sailors with poets. I am no bookworm and have read little poetry, but I know that poets manage to escape from the grey reality of everyday life to a world created by vivid imagination; dreamers, they follow an ideal which yields no pecuniary profit. Without a considerable sense of poetry you cannot confront the discomfort, exhaustion and danger of a climb — particularly on a big face — nor a life at sea. Climbers, sailors and poets all strive to evade the monotonous sequence of identical days and risk the unknown, driven on by an unbridled passion. It is certainly true, though, that on a section of hard climbing there is no time to dream, and every movement must be calculated to within a millimetre: you reach for the extremes of possibility, the ultimate limit of the laws of gravity, without exceeding or breaking the delicate balance, for otherwise you fall; and a fall is always unpleasant. Even if the pitons and rope hold, even if your companions act quickly and correctly, rock is always hard. But there are enforced intervals on a climb, and at these moments the tension subsides and thoughts wander freely, if only for a moment; then images and memories flicker rapidly through the mind.

There are also innumerable aspects of mountains before which the soul of even a less sensitive man trembles astonished; a cloud which, passing in front of the sun, becomes ringed with gold; a ray which pierces the cloud cover to strike the rock like a sword, animating the stone with living colour; the mist driven by the wind up the couloirs, dragging its characteristic smell with it; the vastness of the horizon where scores of peaks stretch away behind each other; the claustrophobia of a Dolomite basin which seems to squeeze the breath out of you; the bivouacs on the face.

The preparations for a bivouac are lengthy, often a race against darkness; but when, having arranged everything, you look for the most comfortable place to sleep — and heaven knows it's nearly always uncomfortable — then in a sense the whole mountain is present in you: you get the feeling of being part of it, and that is poetry too. Each one feels it in his own way, according to diverse habits, desires and personality; but each one of that ill-matched bunch who are real climbers, even though he may not find the means to express what he finds in language, at the bottom of his heart is still a poet even if — especially when young — he finds it shameful to confess.

When Vittorio Ratti and I came back from our ascent of the South-East Ridge of Torre Trieste, one of the climbers who came to shake our hands — I do not remember his name — said:

"On those 700 metres of rock you wrote a poem."

At the time we laughed; but later we realised he was right.

I said earlier that climbing is a thing that you feel in your blood. I, for example, was not born near the mountains: most people think I am from Lecco because I have spent most of my life there, but in fact I am from Savorgagno, a region of San Vito al Tagliamento in lower Friuli. My parents were peasants. I don't remember my father; when I was two he went to America and was killed in an accident at work. My mother and I went to live with my grandfather (he was a peasant too) where, with a handful of maternal aunts, they contrived to bring me up. They say that I was a little terror, forever playing truant from school to go fishing in ditches or pedalling off on my bike along the dusty roads, but you should not believe such calumnies. . . .

At the age of 12 I went to work as a bellows-boy in a blacksmith's shop. Later on the advice of a friend, I moved to Lecco, alone, to look for better work. As soon as I saw the rock faces looming above the city my latent passion for the mountains exploded. Their attraction was so strong that on my first Sunday, with some friends, I climbed the main peak of Resegone, Punta Cermenati. Today, after so many years, I remember that first outing with profound nostalgia: our early morning departure under the stars; our lack of equipment, borrowed rucksack and ancient clothes worn so as not to dirty our better ones; our frantic desire which drove us upwards at a desperate pace, the joy of reaching that first summit . . . Victory! It was the decisive turning point in my life, the beginning of a mountain mania of which I have never been cured.

After that my working days seemed easier, for I spent the whole week dreaming of my return to those high rocks. With my few needs like a room, laundry and food satisfied (or as nearly as possible: at that age the more you eat the hungrier you get). I sent the rest of my money to my mother and dedicated my free time to the mountains.

Two weeks after climbing Resegone, I discovered the Grigna, a marvellous centre for rock climbing, which had been popular for many generations and an area that became very dear to me. On its short but difficult routes I did my early climbs and had the indelible satisfaction of a first ascent

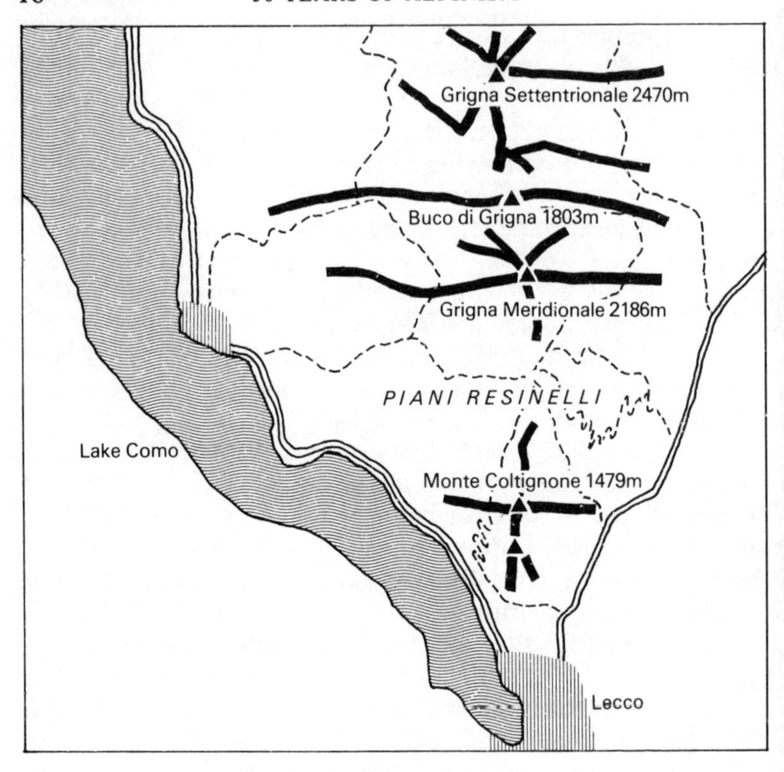

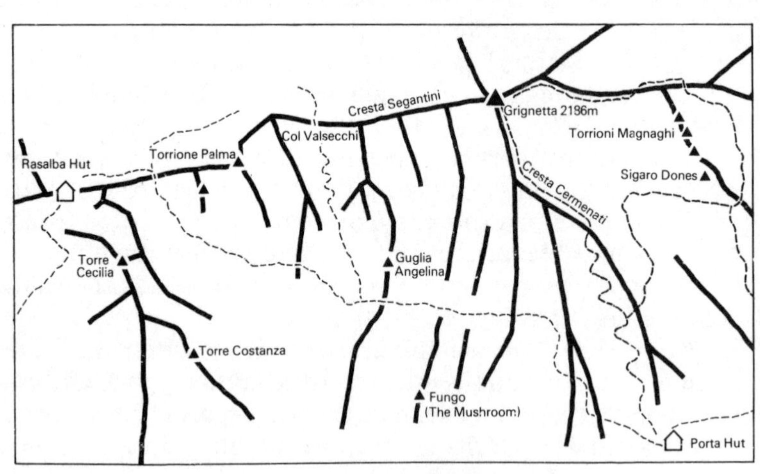

The Grigna Meridionale massif

and a first bivouac. The thrill of returning to those wonderful routes week after week allowed me to live through the hard-working years of my youth.

I did several routes, ranging from easy to more difficult and each one seemed to say something new, yet in a language I already understood. It was a true sensual communication, as if the mountain were a part of me and I, in possessing it, could feel the depth of that correspondence.

Daily sacrifices meant that I could buy my first pair of boots for 75 lire; I gave up boxing, which I enjoyed very much, because climbing was slowing down my muscle reflexes, and self-taxation imposed a burden of five cents monthly for membership of our climbing club, the Nuova Italia. We aimed at first at climbing as many peaks as possible, preferring classic routes and the most accessible one-day routes. I remember our first indispensable pieces of equipment: ropes, karabiners, and homemade pitons, vast and ridiculously heavy compared to modern ones. Our rappels were always made just using the rope, without sling or karabiner or the modern rappel devices.

How it's all changed!

In those days my friends and I could climb only on Sunday or, rarely, on Saturday, and if we were lucky enough to have three days off in a row we were indescribably happy. When we were climbing in the Grigna we could postpone finishing a climb until the next week since it was near home. But when we had to travel far for a climb, we couldn't fail because we only had one chance. Imagine yourself at the base of an unclimbed route, competing against four or five climbing teams for the first attempt, watching your only free days evaporate as fast as mist in a couloir!

It is said that when I jump into an adventure I am pig-headed; I won't give up even when bad weather counsels retreat. The truth of it is that I had so few days for climbing as a youth that I always wanted to make the most of any free time I had. Moreover, in the Dolomites, many important and famous climbers lived at the bases of great climbs. Many of them could take as much time as they wanted on particular climbs and stay in the mountains for months if they liked. It was easy for those lucky climbers to attempt the same route over and over until they succeeded.

In the spring of 1929, the ascent of Guglia Angelina, an elegant pinnacle between the couloirs of Val Tesa and the Valsecchi, was chosen to test our first hemp rope, some 50 metres long. The leader was my friend Mario Dell'Oro, nicknamed Boga, well-known among fellow climbers for his ability. Having reached the first ledge, Boga, who was leading, and Mario Villa, the second man, lost the route because of a sudden thick mist that limited visibility to a couple of metres. Comi and I, who were following, lost sight of them, climbed on without a rope, forced a difficult chimney and reached the top, where Boga and Villa joined us later — rather luckily, for we could then use their rope for the descent.

Even today I wonder how on earth we would have got down and what would have happened, given our limited experience, if our friends hadn't reached the top.

CHAPTER TWO

My First New Routes

1930-1932: Corna di Medale (S.S.E. Face) Guglia Angelina (East Face) Sigaro Dones (North Edge) Sasso dei Carbonari (South East Face) Pizzo della Pieve (North East Face) Pizzo d'Eghen (West Face) Guglia Angelina (West Face)

With careful and continuous practice, our methods improved, and the Grigna rang to the rhythm of our hammers. As our experience in climbing techniques grew I began increasingly to want to concentrate on virgin ground.

In the autumn of 1930, my friend Carlo Corti invited me to make an attempt on the unclimbed South South East Face of the Corna di Medale, an imposing and forbidding wall, with many overhangs, some 400 metres high, overlooking Malevedo, a suberb of Lecco. It was filthy and vegetated, more like virgin forest than rock, and Corti got the brunt of it. we traversed gently leftwards towards a vertical diedre, climbed that and came to a ledge, about halfway up the face, where we could rest, eat and drink. Then we went on, passing the high point reached by previous parties, though that didn't matter particularly to us: what mattered was the summit, still far above us. We were confident of reaching it that day as we were not at all tired and there were hours of daylight left.

Climbing a chimney, I was about 15 metres above Corti and had placed two pitons when a hold that promised to be solid turned out to be a loose chockstone. As I pulled up on it, it moved, pulled out, and came down on top of me. By rights that should have been the end of me: it broke in two and one half knocked my other hand off the rock while the other half smashed against my knee. I lost what remained of my balance and went flying: rock whizzed past my eyes, then bushes, then my friend, then rock again; I felt the jerk of the rope and found myself hanging in space, bouncing over a 200 metre drop. It had all happened so fast that I hadn't had time to be afraid.

It was my first fall, and it had been a long one because one of my top pitons had pulled out. My forehead, nose and left hand were streaming blood, and my right knee was so badly smashed that I was immobilised for two weeks. It was the end of climbing for that year.

The following year I met Mary Varale, who was to become famous in 1933 for her first ascent of the Yellow Edge on Cima Piccola di Lavaredo with Emilio Comici and Renato Zanutti. On July 2, 1931 Mary and I made the first ascent of the East Face of Guglia Angelina, an interesting Grade 4 route with some Grade 5 moves, which takes an extremely exposed face. Mary was an exceptional companion, alert, ready and utterly trustworthy. In the weeks preceding our climb on the Guglia Angelina we had done a number of repeat ascents together and were completely in tune with each other.

The route was tortuous, a series of discontinuous rising traverses zigzagging across the face, requiring a good deal of time and care on the delicate moves and friable rock. After an overhang and a chimney we reached the top. The feeling was unforgettable: I felt as if I had given life to those rocks, which until then had been touched only by the sun and the wind.

It is perhaps worth noting that by that time we had begun to use pitons for direct aid — earlier they had been used only for belays and running belays. As the gap between the old and these new methods of climbing widened, it caused great and lively debates between the old and new generations of climbers.

Later that month, on July 26, with Giovanni Riva ('Sora') I climbed the North Edge of the Sigaro Dones, the most original and difficult peak in Grigna. It is a monolith surrounded only by a dizzying expanse of air, slender and isolated like a campanile, placed in a wild and fantastic location. Its north side presents a difficult and challenging climb with moves of Grade 5 and 6 many of which were very exposed. By defying all natural laws we fought our way up and, by doing acrobatics on Sora's shoulders, I finally placed a piton in a small crack which had forced us to retreat during an earlier attempt. Our elation on the summit was proportional to the difficulties we had overcome, and I savoured a moment of deep pleasure at the conquest of that elegant overhanging wall. The descent was by rappel: three continuous pitches down the same route, down into the spinning void.

I could only climb on Sundays, and the next free day that I had after the Sigaro conquest, I returned with Boga to attempt the South South East Face of the Corna di Medale — the climb that had previously defeated me. We had soon passed my previous high point and were so absorbed in the characteristic cracks and overhangs that we didn't notice the deteriorating weather. We were about two-thirds of the way up the face when the black clouds met and ominous peals of thunder were soon followed by great drops of rain that hit us as hard as stones. Lightning struck the ridge, and the rain came down in torrents. Our descent rapidly assumed the character of a flight. We had noticed a sheltered niche on the way up and tucked ourselves into it; Boga poked his head out and pronounced with dignity:

"If it's coming down this hard it won't last long."

In the morning we climbed on, by now certain of success. first we overcame a diagonal traverse to the left, then climbed up a slender chimney to a very steep corner. Here an enormous overhanging monolith seemed to block our way, but a crack allowed us to go to the right where the monolith leaned against the wall, to reach a corner that led to the top.

1931 ended happily with another first ascent, on September 20. With Riccardo Redaelli I made a climb on the South West Face of the Torrione Palma (Palma Tower) in the southern section of the Grigna. The face, which looks towards the Piramidi Casati, gave us a challenging Grade 4 free-climb.

While awaiting the new rock climbing season, I took an active part in winter and spring ski races. These were mostly ski-touring races: in those days ski lifts did not exist. Carrying my skis I would climb for three or four hours to reach the Castelli hut in Artavaggio, then to the Lecco hut in Bobbio, or to Grassi del Camisolo, the highest hut, or to the Pizzo dei

Tre Signori, or in Pialeral under the Grignone. Such strenuous exercise proved to be valuable training for my next climbs.

1932 proved to be another good year. On July 8, Boga and I made a new route on the South East Face of Sasso dei Carbonari, between Val Meria and the Conca di Releccio, an imposing face more than 500 metres high. It is named after the charcoal burners who used to work below it. We attacked it one clear morning, our previous trepidation forgotten as, in the wild solitude, we gazed in silence at the huge wall. We led through on the whole climb and even though we had trained for the route separately we climbed together perfectly as a team for the first time that year.

After following a steep gully for about 50 metres, we reached a wide grassy ledge which cut across the wall. Here we traversed up to the right and found the next 30 metres very difficult, with so few holds that we had to use pitons. I then led up a slightly overhanging crack on almost non-existent holds for about 25 metres. This section and a section directly under the summit were the most difficult of the whole route. The moves, which we climbed without protection, were all about Grade 5.

We felt tremendously relaxed when we reached the summit, our satisfaction merging with the happiness of our friends, both male and female, who had come up the ordinary route to meet us and bring food. On Grigna a cloud sat like a great cap, streaming out towards Valsassina. Someone started singing. These were happy moments when we felt aware of our youthfulness — full of enthusiasm and hope.

On July 20, Boga and I teamed up with Giuseppe Comi to make a new route on the North East Face of Pizzo della Pieve, the last rampart of the great rocky ridge of the northern Grigna. Our friend Comi, now our official photographer, came armed with a vast camera and great professional enthusiasm.

The gentle pastoral aspect of the South East Face is in vivid contrast to the North East Face which is characterised by vertical slashes, slabs and gullies. The face is commonly called 'La Fasana' after Eugenio Fasana, who made the first ascent. It is a grand formation that at some points reaches the height of 800 metres. We had spotted our intended route while making an ascent of Fasana's route the previous year.

I treasure a fond memory of the custodian of the Pialeral Hut, from which we started early in the morning. Having intuitively understood and foreseen our intentions, he gave us extra milk and coffee as his contribution to the success of our project. Sandy-eyed with lack of sleep, we set out as the first light reflected on the dew, disturbing a herd of mountain goats. They perched on a rock watching us, idly scratching their backs with their horns to express their disdain.

The start of the climb consisted of 100 metres of smooth slabs, followed by a loose gully and some 30 metres of very loose rock. At this point the wall presented its main difficulties. The smoothness of the great slabs to the right was discouraging so, with Boga leading, we moved left and followed a crack of continuous difficulty. We continued, switching leads, until I was confronted by a six-metre rocky rib. This proved to be the most tricky part of the climb. I had difficulty in placing a piton and this delayed me for some time, after which I reached a belay spot and brought up my companions. We moved to the right a little, circumventing an overhang, and this manoeuvre led us to a well-defined shoulder. The natural way in which we had arrived at this good point confirmed that we had followed the most logical route. Although the route-finding had provided some interest, the climbing hadn't been particularly difficult, the rocky rib being the only section of Grade 5.

The next Sunday, Corti and I made a new Grade 4 route on the West Face of the Pizzo d'Eghen. The 'Point', as it is called, is the northern spur of the Palono, itself a branch of the Grigna. We left on Saturday night from Lecco on bicycles, reaching Cortabbio at midnight. We slept at a friend's house and by 4 a.m., brisk as little fishes, we set out. It was a two-hour walk through dense woods dominated by towering crags; prisoners in that wild beauty, we gazed up at the huge apparition glowering down at us. It was a mean angry barricade, gloomy with shadows, some 500 metres high and riven by a great chimney that started about 200 metres up and ran vertically to the top.

The lower part was at an easy angle but the chimney itself, dank and vegetated, was steeper and was characterised by a number of constrictions and niches capped by overhangs. There were five of these: we avoided the first, climbed straight over the second with a couple of pitons and made a human pyramid to get over the third, much to Corti's disgust. "You know you climb just like an elephant," he said as I found a good foothold on his head.

Above the fourth overhang, on a ledge, we made a cairn to commemorate our visit. This good intention — to reassure teams repeating the route — came to nothing as it was 25 years before the route was climbed again and by then our cairn, a veritable work of art, had vanished.

Above, the steep crack, which seemed to want to jettison us out into space, widened again and we had to change our tactics. Finally we emerged at the top to a familiar landscape. Hungry as wolves, we made for the Monza Hut, dreaming of great mounds of spaghetti or risotto. But it was closed. We collapsed, exhausted and starving, and fell asleep. . . .

Hours later we stumbled our way down to Cortabbio, loosing the path again and again in the dark. Our torch died; Corti, leaping from rock to rock across the river in his nailed boots, fell headlong into the water, to my delight and his fury, and we pedalled back to Lecco at breakneck speed, desperate for food.

In late autumn, on October 28, Boga, Mary Varale and I ended the 1932 season with a new Grade 4 route on the West Face of Guglia Angelina.

At the Porta Hut, which, contrary to habit, we reached a night early, we met various friends who had come to welcome Signora Varale who was already a well-known climber. In response to our demands she promised us all that she would bring Emilio Comici over to Grigna next Spring.

Early the next morning we climbed the trail, leaving it under the face of Ago Teresita. A ledge led us to 'Hell's Door', a *breche* which is located on a crumbling arête. From start to finish the tension was almost continuous because of the great exposure. Boga, all cool nerve and strength, led with ease and style, climbing methodically, evaluating the route, and choosing good holds. As the last on the rope, I enjoyed watching my friend climbing with so much agility.

From a fork in the rock he moved diagonally, crossing a section of crumbling rock; in a long, delicate traverse, we arrived at the top of a dangerous wall and reached another ledge. Keeping to the left, we found a groove with a crack at the top of which was an open gully. After a last small overhang, we were on top.

It was an arduous route that simultaneously proposed and resolved a problem that was becoming topical in those years: the search for more difficult routes on faces that had already been climbed. This inevitably necessitated using pitons for aid as well as protection, which displeased a lot of climbers. They said that our pitons "polluted and wounded the mountain's sacred body" and that we were "laddermakers" ignorant of mountaineering ethics. Later it grew worse: they said it was the end of climbing, as if the end derived from evolution and change rather than this desperate clinging to the past.

CHAPTER THREE

Encounter with the Dolomites

1932: Ascents in the Brenta A meeting with Tita Piaz
Traverse of the Vajolet Towers

During the evenings, which I spent in our club centre, or during rests in huts either before or after a climb, I often talked with my friends about the famous Dolomites. We flipped through magazines, commenting on photographs that illustrated that fantastic kingdom of towers, ridges and pinnacles. We were desperately keen to visit them and climb them, but it was a difficult dream to realize.

While returning from a training session on the trail of the 'direttissima' in the Grigna area, on the Sunday following our success on the Pizzo della Pieve, my friend Riccardo Redaelli asked me to go with him to the Dolomites during a week's vacation. He didn't have to ask me twice: the sudden realization of my dream made me wild with delight.

Maybe all this is behind me today, or at least has a different meaning. During my life I have often been able to do what I want; but in those days a week's vacation earned after a full year's hard work, plus the appealing prospect of spending it in the Dolomites, increased the value of something which was already very precious for me and gave me a feeling of profound wellbeing.

I remember our frenetic preparations: the multiplicity of climbing plans, the lists of indispensable equipment, our nerve-racked anxiety as we waited to leave, the car journey made at night to save valuable climbing time.

Riding up from Pinzolo to the Madonna di Campiglio, the fantastic sight of the Brenta Dolomites transfigured by rosy pink in the first dawn light, the intense scent of the pines and the fields of rhododendrons filled my eyes and my heart, while the actual sight of the mountains served to magnify my gigantic desire to climb them: here reality was superior to dreams!

Redaelli had been to the Dolomites before, so we wasted no time. Kiene's route on Castelleto, the classic route and the Fehrmann route on the Campanile Basso and the Piaz Chimney on the Croz del Rifugio were my first contacts with the Brenta — the so-called pale mountains. On these first climbs I confess that I was dumbfounded by the indescribable thrust of those Dolomite pinnacles.

We continued to Trento and here I had the great good fortune to be given a pair of authentic klettershue with felt soles. We drove on towards the Catinaccio group with our full packs of provisions. The extraordinary beauty of the landscape was enhanced by the sunset which created a strong contrast between the dark forest and the flaring red of the peaks. At the Catinaccio I was delighted to meet Tita Piaz, who was at that time the custodian of the Vajolet Hut, and was both proud and a trifle embarrased when he said, "I have heard of you." I was struck by his personal style, his simple mannerisms and incisive words. We seemed to develop an immediate and cordial rapport which resulted in an understanding between a famous old guide and me, still a young boy. I grew to admire his limitless love for mountains, his youthful spirit and his modesty about his own routes, his innovations in climbing techniques. Our climb over the Vajolet Towers started from the slender Torre Delago, and continued with the second ascent of Punta Emma by the Piaz Route under the vigilant eye of the great master. It represented a rich experience of sensations, memories, teachings and hopes for the future. He was not there when we called on our way home; he was always on the move, a perpetual-motion man.

Piaz was renowned for charging some of his clients astronomical sums, but young climbers with no money and plenty of promise he taught free. Anecdotes about the 'Dolomite Devil' abounded; some were true, others were doubtless apocryphal, but together they gave a vivid impression of this capricious and inspired mountaineer whose speech and climbing recognised no limits. I met him only once more, years later, a few days before he died in a motorcycle smash; we had corresponded regularly in the intervening period, mostly about climbing, but I had no chance to speak to him until after the war when, passing his house on the way down from the Catinaccio, I knocked on his door. He was at his desk, awash in a veritable sea of litter.

"Who is it?" he called.

When he heard my name he leapt up, crying in his singsong Trento dialect:

"Eh, so what brings you to these parts? You know it really does me good when somebody remembers poor old me."

Everybody remembered him, as he knew perfectly well, but denying it was a game that amused him. Despite my protests he shot off to the wine shop and came back with a bottle that he thrust at me.

"Drink!" he ordered.

I barely drink wine, and then only at mealtimes, but you couldn't argue with Tita. We stayed drinking for hours, talking of mountains and men and then mountains again, swinging from agreement to difference and back, with Tita, volcanic as ever, embellishing every tale with curses interspersed with eulogy. He showed me the manuscript of a book he was writing but whipped it out of my hand immediately:

"Hell, you can read that when it's published; let's talk now."

What was striking about him was not only his youthfulness but also his immeasurable love for mountains, a lifelong dedication which had not gone unrewarded: mountains are never ungrateful. Always ready to help anyone in danger, he never liked to talk about his numerous rescues, changing the subject quickly; about his innovations he was more expansive, though there was never any self-aggrandisement. He merely liked to reminisce about them because they reminded him of his younger days and gave him the satisfaction that any artist has when looking back on his greatest works.

CHAPTER FOUR

New Techniques Happily put to Use

1933-1934: Comici visits the Grigna Zuccone de Campelli (West Face)
Corno del Nibbio (East Face) Torre Costanza (East Face)
Cima Ovest (Dulfer Route) Cinque Torre (Dimai Route)
Torre del Diavollo (Comici Route) Sasso Cavallo (South Face)
Torre Costanza (East Face) Corno del Nibbio (East Face—2nd Route)
Pizzo della Pieve (North East Face—2nd Route)
Cimone della Bagozza (North Spur)

Mary Varale kept her promise, turning 1933, which had already started well*, into an exceptional year by bringing Comici to Grigna. Emilio Comici, that perfectionist of style, regarded climbing as a form of art, comparing its harmonies with those of a piece of music whose rhythms and movements must adapt themselves to the quality and roughness of rock. Comici was already famous for the breadth of vision inherent in his various routes. He was considered the ultimate stylist, not only in his climbing, but also for his choice of line. This was always the nearest possible to a direct route up a face, epitomized by his celebrated dictum:

> I wish someday to make a route and from the summit let fall a drop of water and this is where my route will have gone.

To be able to listen to him, to be advised by him, to absorb his philosophy was a rare stroke of luck for us. We thought him a master; always available, always kind, he was from the start very supportive, acting simply with the kind of camaraderie that almost always exists between mountaineers.

The idea of artificial climbing, which we were not yet practising, and the first-hand view of Dolomite techniques demonstrated by Comici, found fertile ground in me and the members of our group. He was able to show us the recent

* Earlier in the year I had teamed up with Cariboni Rizieri to make the first ascent of the great crack that cleaves the South East Face of the Torrione Magnaghi Central — a sustained Grade 4 chimney and crack climb.

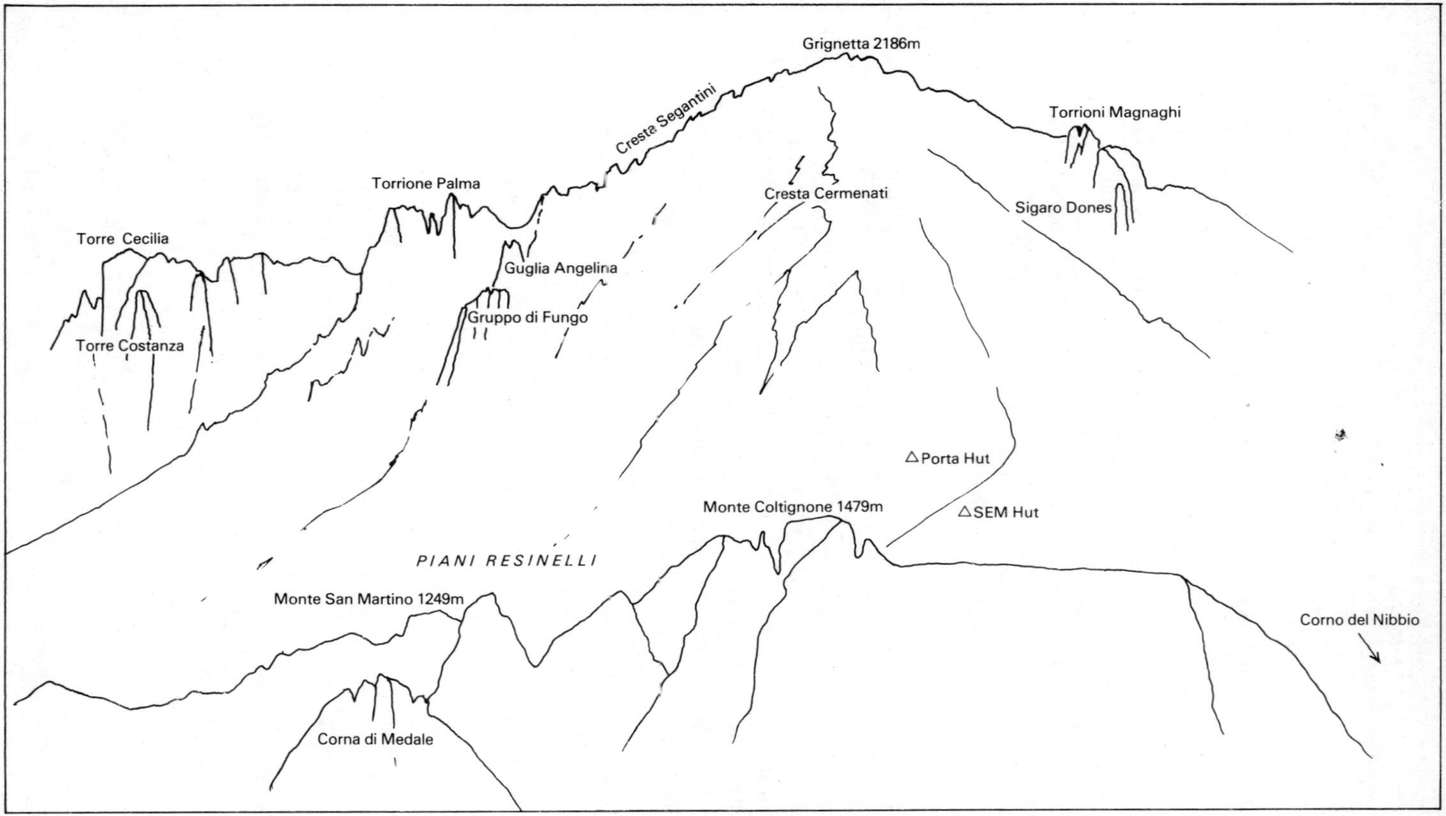

1 The Grigna Meridionale massif seen from Monte Coltignone

2 The young Cassin — a keen boxer before climbing captured his interest.

3 Cassin and Mary Varale after the Guglia Angelina ascent in July 1931.

4 Guglia Angelina (Grigna Meridionale) with the Cassin/Varale Route marked. The Gruppo di Fungo is in the lower left corner of the picture and the high alp of the Piani Resinelli is beyond, with the deep trench of the Como/Lecco valley in the distance.

5 Mario Dell'Oro (nicknamed Boga) poses with Cassin after their ascent of the South South East Face of Corna di Medale in August 1931.

6 Cassin and friend race up to the Grigna for a Sunday's climbing in the summer of 1932. Torre Costanza is the pinnacle in the distance.

7 Sigaro Dones (Grigna Meridionale) with the North Ridge marked. This difficult climb (Grade 5 and 6) was first climbed by Cassin and Giovanni Riva in July 1931.

8 The Lecco climbers with the President of the Italian Alpine Club (CAI) Angelo Manaresi when he visited the Grigna in 1932. Left to right (mainly in front row): Giovanni Carnati (behind girl), Antonio Spreafico (in sleeveless sweater), Mario Dell'Oro (Boga), Annibale Ravasi (President of the Lecco Section of the CAI), Manaresi, Cassin, Giovanni Riva, Antonio Piloni (white shirt/black sweater) and Giovanni Valsecchi (extreme right, not the [illegible]

9 (left) The 1932 Cassin/Comi Route (Grade 4) on the East Face of Pizzo d'Eghen.

10 (right) The 1934 Cassin/Pozzi Route (Grade 4) on the East Face of Torre Cecilia (Grigna Meridionale).

11 The Corno del Nibbio with the Comici Route (left) and the two subsequent Cassin routes marked.

13 Sasso Cavallo and Sasso dei Carbonari in the Grigna Settentrionale group.

14 Tita Piaz — "We climbed under the vigilant eye of the great master".

15 Emilio Comici who made the tantalizing pronouncement that "we were ready for any climb in the Dolomites".

16 Cassin in action on the South East Face of the central peak of Torrione Magnaghi (Grigna Meridionale).

17 Emilio Comici (centre), with Cassin and Dell'Oro (Boga), during his visit to the Grigna in 1933.

18 Members of the Lecco Mountain Rescue Team at Resegone in 1932 for the ceremony of blessing the equipment. Those present include: 1. Luigi Sacchi, 2. Sebastiano Pozzi, 3. Bruno Citterio, 4. Giuseppe Comi, 5. Antonio Piloni, 6. Giuseppe Perego, 7. Battista Riva, 8. Annibale Ravasi, 9. Carlo Suzoini, 10. Giuseppe Giudici (Farfallino), 11. Giovanni Riva (Sora), 12. Mario Spreafico (Umet), 13. Mario Dell'Oro (Boga), 14. Giovanni Rusconi, 15. Riccardo Cassin, 16. Colombo, 17. Ugo Tizzoni.

refinements of the eastern alpine school, information which had recently become available in Italy thanks to Domenico Rudatis, who had kept in constant contact with the German school of the Kaisergebirge, at that time the *avant-garde* of rock climbing. But although we were very open to innovation, we realized at the same time that as far as free climbing was concerned Comici had little to teach us.

On the Corno del Nibbio, Comici led a new route on which he demonstrated double rope technique and the use of etriers. This was the first time these techniques had been used in the Grigna. By watching him closely we intuitively understood the economy of movement and energy saving possibilities of these methods. Then with Comici, Mary Varale, Mario Spreafico and Boga, evenly divided on two ropes, I took part in the ascent of the northern crack of the West Face of Zuccone de Campelli, a new and elegant route on the smooth lakeside slopes between Valsassina and Val Torta which goes from the scree slopes of the Chamois valley directly to the summit: it required getting over a difficult crack, with awkward route-finding and overhanging in several places.

Having completed nine new climbs with us and numerous classical second ascents, Comici made the tantalising pronouncement; we were "ready for any climb in the Dolomites."

These climbs led to my having a warm and long-lasting friendship with Comici which grew with the passage of time and has left me with a store of wonderful memories and a warmth that cannot be forgotten. A typical example of this friendship was an incident that happened a few months later during our summer holidays in the Dolomites. Antonio Piloni and I were making the second ascent of one of Comici's routes. He must have been watching us from the woods below for when we were starting our descent, rappeling on the doubled rope, a warning drifted up on the resin-scented breeze: "the rope doesn't reach!" We couldn't see anyone and there was nobody around when we got to the bottom, but I knew that this way of intervening at the moment of need, yet keeping out of the limelight, was absolutely Comici's style.

Comici's groove route on the East Face of Corno del Nibbio had fired us with determination to add our own route to the wall which was after all in our home territory — the Grigna. Up till this time less than half of our first ascents had been among the numerous spires of the Grigna, a situation that now clearly needed correction. Our line went to the right of that taken by Comici whose route occupied the centre of the face. We took a line up an overhanging wall, split diagonally by deep cracks of varying widths. I was accompanied on this climb by Antonio Piloni and Augusto Corti. The climbing difficulties were sustained at Grade 5 with one Grade 6 passage in a narrow and overhanging crack, where we appreciated to the full the advantages of artificial climbing and the use of etriers.* We were euphoric over this new victory, not only because it was a beautiful route, but because it gave us a thorough work-out with the new techniques we had just learned.

After the Nibbio success, Antonio Piloni, Domenico Lazzeri and I solved the problem of the South Face of the Torre Costanza, the most powerful monolith of the Grignetta in Val Tesa. We knew it would be difficult, but we were determined to win on this Grade 6 route, which even today is considered one of the most challenging of the area.

I led off, cutting to the right of a slope of grass and rock that ran all the way to the ledge from the base. After climbing a rather steep crack, I got on top of Piloni's shoulders and immediately started placing pitons up to a leaning triangular niche with a groove which I gained with a very delicate move. I then climbed an overhanging and extremely difficult crack on the left: there were plenty of good piton placements but the climbing was continually exposed.

A providential stop on a grass-covered ledge, a rich oasis in the middle of the sunbaked wall, restored us, but we soon moved on knowing that many more difficult pitches awaited us. First there was a smooth slab, then a dark overhanging chimney that closed at the top and was very exposed. Above this the climb continued as a crack which eventually deepened again into a chimney. Progress was slow but continuous. I

* The etrier then consisted of a simple rope ring with various knots that tightened on and constricted the foot.

placed a few necessary pitons while my companions manoeuvred the ropes one by one. The wall now overhung so much that a falling rock wouldn't have hit them, 15 metres below, but would have fallen directly to the base of the tower. The exposure was marvellous — totally intoxicating.

At the last great difficulty, where the chimney again closed and the rock overhung decisively, I needed the help of pitons and etriers to get under the overhang. Standing suspended on the rim, I placed a piton and managed to overcome all the obstacles.

At the summit I brought up my friends with considerable effort. Lazzeri, since he was last, became prey to gravity every time he unclipped from a karabiner, swinging out over the monstrous drop on our ancient frayed rope. By the time he reached the top we were all drenched in sweat.

In the holidays of 1933 the eastern Dolomites were the goal of our Nuova Italia club. We pitched our tents a little above Lake Misurina in magnificent countryside where the crystal clarity of the lake, the majesty of the mountains, the forests, sweet-scented lillies and all the other flowers combined in a scene of enchanting beauty. My heart pounded with anticipation of the pleasures to come climbing in these fabulous peaks. Thus, Piloni and I repeated the entertaining Dülfer Route on the Cima Ovest, then the Comici Route on the Torre del Diavolo; to finish our short vocation, we went to the Cinque Torre to do the Dimai brothers' route on the east crack of the South Peak, where the existing piton after the great overhang (most useful for pulling oneself out) played a terrible trick on me and let me experience real terror for the first time. Having clipped in a karabiner, I grabbed the rope with one hand to get up and as soon as I was on top of the piton I felt and saw it, and the karabiner, sliding gently down the rope. I did not have time to control my moves; when I found myself on top of the overhang my heart was hammering and breathing was difficult.

Back at the Grigna, the South Face of Sasso Cavallo was our next objective. This was a 400 metre wall, with many overhangs in its lower section, then rearing up in a vertical face. It was remote and had therefore remained unclimbed. My first attempt with Piloni, when we reached a good point high on the route, was cut short by lack of time. After that Piloni had to work on Sundays: with a sigh, he told me to get on with it, so it was with Augusto Corti that I went up to the Elisa Hut the following Saturday night.

In the early dawn of August 31, we attacked. It was a gorgeous day and knowing the route for a good distance saved us a lot of time. The difficulties that day are indelibly stamped in our memories and, even after many years, it is enough to think about that climb for just one second to be able to envision one particular crack, this overhang, that fixed piton at that exact moment.

Before noon we got to the highest point of the previous attempt. At that point I was committed to a crack that from the beginning was very exposed and exhausting, which presented two overhangs higher up. After the first I saw the real difficulties. I was now confronted by an extremely difficult section of climbing. There were hardly any holds and I would obviously have to make progress by further use of pitons. Yet the rock was smooth, compact and crackless; there was not even the slightest of faults that might take a piton. Moreover the situation was serious as Corti was belayed below on an assortment of very dubious pitons. I tried and tried to place a piton until my hair was dripping with sweat, but finally I could not resist the thought that had been hammering away at me as I had hammered the piton:

"I'll have to stop," I called down, preparing to retreat.

"You can't!" Corti roared.

He was right. I had no choice but to keep trying.

Not retreating from this obstacle was an exercise in sheer will-power. Somehow I managed to make progress. I remember with vivid clarity each detail of the obdurate rock, the sweaty piton finally hammered in, the second overhang which, though easier than the first, still required some delicate manoeuvres. At that point there was another crisis — Corti called to me that there was no more rope and there was nowhere to stop.

"Come up about a metre," I called down, "so that I can reach somewhere to belay"

After another 60 metres of smooth wall, slightly overhanging, with crackless rock that stubbornly rejected pitons, we found a gully to follow and finally emerged at the top. We were early and allowed ourselves a brief rest. The fading colours, the late afternoon, the short stop after an entire day full of emotions: these mould one's entire being. Absorbed in the enjoyment of these moments, so rich in intimate sensations, we felt no need to talk; but a rooster in the valley below destroying the calm with an unexpected burst of crowing, inviting us to descend.

On the morning of October 15, I set out from the Porta Hut with Mary Varale and Boga, towards Costanza. The frosty fields signalled the imminent arrival of the cold season, the forest with its warm autumn colours, the pale sun occasionally illuminating the summit of the Grignetta which, wrapped in fog, threw up a swirling display of dark shadows, gave everything a cold and impenetrable air, in contrast to our vivid enthusiasm to conquer the East Face of Torre Costanza.

Mary had tried it with Comici and Augusto Corti the previous spring, but their attempt had been cut short with a piton pulled out and Comici took a fall. Since then Mary had been obsessed with the idea of climbing it, and had mentioned it again and again to Corti and me.

We attacked the cold, damp rock, with me in the lead, followed by Mary and Boga, and soon reached the spot where the real difficulties begin: one of those barely-visible cracks characteristic of the Grignetta. Mary confirmed that the pitons I found at that point were those of the previous attempt, and with their help I placed others and crawled up to where the rock bulged out like a great belly, where I traversed to the left. I took a belay and Mary followed climbing with perfect technique.

After about ten very exposed metres of Grade 5 climbing, I took another stance and brought up Mary. There was not enough room for all of us so I moved up a little to make room for Boga. The major difficulties over, we reached the summit on pleasant rock, finding enough wind up there to clear away the mist. Mary, delighted and typically open-hearted, awarded us each a kiss.

It was our last climb of 1933, and we were satisfied; but already we were dreaming of famous routes and unsolved problems for the next year, even though we would not reveal them.

"Who hasn't got plans?" Mary sighed, clearly fishing for ours.

"The important thing is to realise them," Boga replied enigmatically, refusing to be drawn.

In the spring of 1934, I climbed a new Grade 4 route with Luigi Pozzi on the West Face of Torre Cecilia, on which I had done all the routes. The enthusiasm of my young friend on his first new route gave me great pleasure: reflected in him. I saw my very own feelings when I ventured for the first time on to virgin territory.

On the Corno del Nibbio, a very popular training ground for rock-climbing, I picked out another new line on the East Face, a little south of the one I climbed the previous year with Piloni and Corti. It seemed more technical than the preceding climb because it went straight up and, overall, was much steeper. The difficulties were considerable all the way to the top, with several sections of Grade 6. The little overhangs that bulge out were the most characteristic and salient points in the first pitch of this climb.

On the second pitch Boga and I satisfied young Panzeri, an agile climber, by letting him take the lead. He was one of our apprentices, and was proud to be climbing with us old-timers, even though we were hard to please. It was beautiful to watch him climbing with such style and elegance.

"There's another hot shot," I muttered to Boga as we were coming down from the summit, driven on by the unexpected and freezing rain that implacably accompanied us all the way down to the hut.

"That's all right; we'll let him buy the beer," said Boga.

Following the dictates of the new ideology of modern alpine climbing, which encourages the practice of always looking for better lines on walls where other routes already exist, Augusto Corti and I added another new route, a direttissima, to the North East Face of the Pizzo della Pieve on July 1, 1934. This was the 'La Fasana' face which Boga, Corti and I had climbed in 1932. Our new line, like the previous one, attacked the cliff directly and continued for one small pitch to a small overhang, after which it went straight up the face until near the top.

I gained access to the base of the wall with a really interesting move that made me positively euphoric. From this position I was able to scrutinise the route and work out the next moves. The overhanging slabs were heavily impressive, intensified by the sullen bleakness surrounding me and the total absence of sound. I recall the oppressive heat and the feverish thirst I suffered during the first pitch.

There followed a series of Grade 5 pitches, but as we got closer to the top the climbing eased to Grade 3 though it still required concentration as the rock was very loose. Most of the climb went free; we used only 12 pitons.

For some time Aldo Frattini, a good friend and trustworthy climbing partner on many second ascents, had been trying to interest me in the North Spur of Cimone della Bagozza, which is in the Camino group between the Camonica Valley and the Scalve Valley. This is a superb 400 metre buttress. At that time it had resisted numerous attempts to climb it by many excellent climbers, the main problem being a 20 metre overhanging rib at about half height. Aldo's driving enthusiasm for the project finally won me round to the idea of "taking a look".

With his famous Kiribiri, a 509 Fiat convertible (a very prestigious automobile at that time), Frattini picked me up in Lecco, and with Rodolfo Varallo we reached Schilpario in the dark. I recall our departure at crack of dawn, a noisy affair as the Kiribiri would not start at any price, the festive look of the lush greens in the fields and forests of our approach march, the painful scree-slope up to the attack point, my avid curiosity about the overhanging rib. The impressiveness of the buttress exceeded all my hopes despite the extravagant hyperbole that I had heard so often. We obviously had to take a closer look. . . .

The first 180 metres succumbed to free climbing with pitons used only for protection. The rock was rather crumbly but the climbing overall was not particularly difficult. After about two hours we reached the major obstacle and the key to the whole ascent: a totally exposed edge of very smooth rock bulging out above us. It was clearly impossible to attack it directly so I tried an outflanking movement, utilizing a steep couloir on the left. After about two hours struggling with this diversion, I managed to gain a point just two metres from the rib above the steep section, but I just couldn't reach it. I then realised that the only solution to the problem was on the improbably overhanging rock on the right, which I had previously discarded because it looked so hard.

The wall was very exposed and very smooth but it was now abundantly clear that if I was to succeed I would have to climb it — some 30 metres of Grade 6. The solution lay with pitons and after two hours of exhausting hammering, I placed eight pitons and had managed to reach a point near the rib and above the overhanging section. Varallo, who came up last, was unable to retrieve all of the pegs. He was the least fit of the three of us and therefore became the scape-goat; but he tolerated our constant grumblings philosophically:

"So today it's my turn. Well, I'll repay you when it's yours," he muttered, adding: "with interest."

Returning to the edge of the spur I climbed for about 70 metres to an inclined ledge at the base of a 25 metre wall. This appeared to be simple but it ended up taking several pitons. A compact and yellowish overhang followed, forcing another deviation of ten metres of Grade 6 climbing. The rock on this section was very smooth and I was forced to climb onto Frattini's shoulders to reach a crucial hold. I then made an exposed traverse to the right and continued up a groove. Suddenly the difficulties eased and I found that we had succeeded.

At nine o'clock in the evening, after a fifteen-hour climb, we were on the summit. The sun was setting and the clear evening sky was streaked with vermillion. We descended rapidly and bivouaced in a shepherd's hut known to my two friends who knew this area like the backs of their hands.

CHAPTER FIVE

Christening a Bivouac Sac

1934: Cima Piccolissima (South East Face) Cima Piccola (Yellow Edge) Cima Grande (North Face—Comici/Dimai)

In the week of summer vacation of 1934 our group based themselves first at the Col of San'Angelo above Misurina, and later at the Lavaredo Hut below the Tre Cime di Lavaredo. Despite bad weather on the first four days of our holiday, Gigi Vitali, Luigi Pozzi and I made the second ascent of a route done the day before on the Popena by Panzeri, Boga and Giudici. This route took the so-called 'left diedre of the overhangs'.

The onset of good weather encouraged us to take a look at the great north faces of the Lavaredo group — rock walls so imposing and charismatic that they even provoke interest outside the climbing world. I myself harboured a very ambitious dream connected with these walls, but more about that later.

After Vitali and I had returned from looking at the North Face of Cima Grande, we found Pozzi, unemployed, pleading to come with us.

"Of course you can come," Vitali said graciously, and then burst out laughing because we weren't going anywhere.

"Then let's go and do the South East Face of the Piccolissima," I said knowing that there was a possible direct route to be found on that unclimbed wall that bristled with overhangs and roofs.

"It's too late," said Vitali — it was by now late morning.

"Never mind, it's only a short route. Anyway we've got a bivouac sac." We were all itching to baptise our new three-man bivvy sac so we hastily collected some gear and set out.

We attacked the face from the deep gully [Dülfer Couloir] that separates the Picolissima from the Punta di Frida. From here the Piccolissima looms above like a mighty human statue on a pedestal. We traversed to the centre of the wall where the difficulties were immediately evident: even the first two overhangs required our most extreme techniques.

With aid from some pitons I moved diagonally to the right; the moves were slow and considered, and allowed me to reach a big ledge, while Pozzi followed so that I should have more rope. Now an overhanging diedre crack put me to the test, especially in its bulging higher section which took a substantial number of pitons. Finally I found a small resting place about 25 metres above the ledge. I traversed right for a couple of metres and then climbed straight up an overhang. It was still Grade 6 climbing and, suspended between air and sky, I delighted in the position and the satisfaction of having overcome so many challenging obstacles. Then I continued for about ten metres on a smooth slab where the contact with holds was minimal, the exposure fierce, and piton placement desperate. I felt like a mad spider on a wall, frantically looking for attachment points for her web.

From a tiny ledge, one of many on the face but too small for the three of us together, I climbed a five metre overhanging groove up to a crack that cut the face horizontally at a formidable overhang, which seemed to preclude the continuation of the new route. Difficulties and problems constantly arose because the face seemed to have been designed upside-down. one fierce test-piece followed another; in retrospect I have no desire to go back there. Due to the smoothness of the rock and the great exposure, I climbed with minimum protection until, moving to the left, I reached a diedre and finally a small ledge, where I could rest for a while after climbing to my limit for such a continuous stretch.

There followed a stretch of Grade 5, then some Grade 4, and finally the three of us were reunited on a spacious ledge. There was still one more Grade 6 section to be climbed but the certainty of success had reinvigorated us and we made short work of that.

Our friends, including the guides Giuseppe Dimai and Innerkoffler, had been following our progress from below. "A short, but logical route that maintains its difficulty at Grade 6," they noted.

It was already evening when we descended from the windy summit to find a spot to bivouac. This was the long-awaited test for our bivouac sac. It was large and new and we were dreaming of a warm, well-deserved rest. Our friends bellowed and, hearing our reassuring voices echoing back from the Frida face, went to sleep in their tents. But the baptism of our bivouac sac was a farce. Pozzi produced a can of salmon from his sac as a glorious treat, but it resisted all our attempts to open it until he resorted to using a piton, spraying all of us and our virgin sac with a stinking liquid which was followed by distinctly unappreciative comments.

In the early morning we went down to the camp site and, the following day, after giving ourselves a few hours' rest, Vitali and I completed, in eight hours (then a record), what was I think the fourth or fifth ascent of the climb completed the previous year by Comici, Mary Varale and Zanutti on the Yellow Edge of Cima Piccola. It is a stupendous and elegant route, as direct and perfect as the maestro himself. On the south corner below the summit, it goes straight up from one overhang to the next.

Our return was permeated by a sense of sadness at the thought of leaving. Boga, too, was depressed because we had been unable to realise our much cherished aim to do the first repeat ascent of the Comici/Dimai Route on the North Face of Cima Grande. We discussed it while we waited in Misurina for the bus. Boga had seen a German team on it; the leader was an extremely good climber, he said, but the third was really a novice. They had retreated for the time being but were clearly intent on renewing the attack. Our group decided quickly: Boga, Vitali and I should stay. They loaned us some gear and as soon as the bus left for Lecco, we shouldered our packs and walked back to the hut.

It was still dark when we set out on Tuesday morning for the base of the climb, where we found Raffaele Carlesso and Hans Vinatzer who had the same idea. We let them go first as they were only a party of two, and we followed with me leading. We made good progress and the climb unfolded steadily. On the last traverse before the bivouac, almost at the end of the difficulties, Vitali, who was third on the rope, begged

Boga, who was second, to remove all the runners. I didn't know about it until Boga arrived at the stance and Vitali shouted up to us to secure the rope so that he could pendulum. I was horrified.

"Too late now," Boga shrugged. "Anyway, he finds this sort of thing fun. Ready?"

"Ready!"

Vitali let go, launching himself into space in a gigantic 25-metre pendulum, swinging to and fro until, when he had finally come to rest, he climbed up the rope hand over hand.

We bivouacked on the face, on the same ledge as Carlesso and Vinatzer. It was Boga's bivvy sac so we didn't have to suffer the stink of salmon all night.

CHAPTER SIX

Accident on Monte Civetta

1935: Monte Civetta (North Face—Comici/Benedetti)

For our 1935 holiday we chose the area round the Vazzoler Hut at the southern end of the Civetta Group. Boga and I, responsible for finding the best camp site, left a few days early.

The landscape was savagely beautiful: meadows exploding with flowers of all colours, an incredible variety of pine trees, the wild crumbling needles of Cantoni de Pelsa forming a foreground to Torre Venezia's soaring majesty, glimpses of Cima della Terranova and Cima su Alto. From the other side the bastion of peaks ranging from Cima de'Toni to the Cantoni della Busazza which capped the lot with its stupendous, audacious pillar, the 'Tower of Towers' which, for sheer beauty, cannot be beaten.

While waiting for the group to arrive, Boga and I went to the Coldai Hut to scrutinize the North West Face of the famous Monte Civetta, for we wanted to make a second ascent of the Comici/Benedetti route. Next morning we left a note for our friends and started out to climb. Switching leads, we reached a bivouac site on a very airy ledge where the 'master' Comici had stopped. Our progress had been quite satisfactory despite the time initially lost in climbing up and down for about 150 metres, trying to find the correct route. We were 700 metres up. Incredible moments, unforgettable visions: a flight of rooks announcing the twilight, the lights of Alleghe and the nearby villages glimmering below us, dark emptiness surrounding us, the barely-discernible silhouette of the Marmolada.

At dawn, frozen stiff after a cold, sleepless night, we shivered as on our shadowed face we watched the sunlight flashing off the Marmolada's icefields. We had to climb to keep warm. A long traverse led me to the spot where Comici's notes said 'pitons with etriers'. The overhang ahead was formidably difficult. After great effort I managed to clip in to a piton and hook in an etrier, then pull over the bulge using a vertical hold. To get myself over the entire overhang I had to leave the etrier, climb Dülfer style* and, with my left hand, reach a small hold, hanging on with my right hand. I tested the hold: it seemed sound. Arching my arms and legs, I flung myself out and up, but suddenly the bloody hold collapsed. Because of my push-off I went into a spin, and because of the sudden somersault, my right hand could not hold me. Falling, I hit the wall and grabbed for the ropes, so that I landed on the ledge on my feet. But I hit it so hard that I bounced off it, turned upside down and fell, totally disorientated. Desperately clutching for the ropes with both hands, I felt that the end had come. Then I banged my head on a projecting rock and lost consciousness. When I came to, nothing made sense. I felt as if an iron band were tightening round my aching spine, squeezing my ribs. . . . Then I heard a voice, first far away and then closer, calling my name. I opened my eyes, but everything was spinning around, so I closed them again.

As my head cleared gradually, reality and rationality returned. I was hanging over a frightening 700-metre drop, with an aching head. I opened my eyes and realized I could not, therefore, be dead. I had fallen about 20 metres. The ropes were not parallel, but came together in a V; hence the spinning. Then I realized if the ropes were not parallel it was because the piton had not pulled, and concluded that I must have fallen so far because Boga hadn't held me properly.

My friend was calling down desperately, fearing the worst. Bruised and angry, I grabbed the vertical rope and hauled myself up over the overhang, clinging to the rock first with one hand and then the other. Even to this day I wonder how I was able to do it in that condition!

Boga was as white as a sheet, except for his hands which were scarlet with blood and torn to shreds because of his attempt to break my fall. The rope was smeared with gore.

*Using tension from the rope.

Anger boiling over, I attacked him.

"Why didn't you hold me?" I rasped.

"I couldn't. My hands were too cold," he muttered finally, unwilling to speak. There was a pause, then: "I couldn't see you." Pause. "I thought you'd gone. . . ."

"So you just let me fall?"

"Only for a moment. I couldn't stop you, my hands wouldn't work. Then once I did get a grip I didn't let go."

I could see from the state of his hands that he had not, but even with the drag on the rope, increased by its running through two karabiners, nobody could stop a fall straight away once it had really started.

"You lead; I'm dizzy," I said.

Quiet as a lamb — the only time in his life that he ever was — Boga led for two pitches, but he was not himself; his usual decisiveness, quickness and confidence was missing. He was very slow, uncertain, as if terrified. I was battered from my fall, but my emotional suffering was nothing compared to his. My own horrors had disappeared into unconsciousness when I passed out; his had increased, to the point where he could barely cope with them.

I took over and led the final part of the route taking a new direct line to the top, a variation finish as Comici's route crosses over to join the Solleder at this point. The increased difficulties on this final section rekindled Boga's enthusiasm and sparkle.

On the Solleder Route, two climbers appeared. I asked them who they were and got the answer:

"Hi Riccardo, it's me, Giusto!"

We waited for them on the summit hoping that Giusto Gervasutti could tell us the normal descent route, but it was dark before they reached us.

Even Gervasutti, who was climbing with Lucien Devies, had difficulty in finding the way down, and after a vain attempt we decided to abandon our efforts and set up a bivouac. Our bivouac sac was only big enough for three, so I let them have it first. They said they would take turns being outside, but they all slept so soundly that they never woke up. I was shyer in those days, and too timid to disturb our guests, so I spent the whole night walking up and down, beating my arms and chest to keep warm while my friends wallowed in deep, refreshing sleep.*

*Gervasutti gives a different account of this incident in his book *Gervasutti's Climbs* (page 135). He describes arriving on the summit in thick mist and overtaking Cassin and Dell'Oro on the descent. He also implies that all four climbers spent the night pacing up and down to try to keep warm. *Publisher's note.*

CHAPTER SEVEN

Torre Trieste's South East Ridge

Talking with Gervasutti during the bivouac hours on Civetta, we focussed on past and future climbs. The South East Ridge of Torre Trieste was the subject of our particular attention: Gervasutti described its characteristics and pronounced it formidable and important — the most logical, beautiful and majestic of routes. He spoke with such enthusiasm and authority that he hardened my already strong desire into an irresistible resolve.

Gervasutti had already attempted the ridge but before reaching the point where the Carlesso/Sandri Route bears off to the left, he had been forced to retreat after a fall caused by a poorly placed piton. The route on the ridge goes straight up, following its slender majesty.

At the Coldai Hut, we found friends who had come to hear our news. I immediately talked about the climb on Torre Trieste to Vittorio Ratti. Ratti was taller than me and younger. Only nineteen, he had all the exuberance of a brilliant spring sunrise. Totally devoid of self-consciousness, he would laugh and sing, joke and play; his openness and easy ways made him everybody's friend. He was a complete athlete, with muscles like steel; he was aware of danger but not afraid of it; the previous winter he had won the junior slalom and that spring had been one of the most promising pupils at our school. In short, I had complete faith in him.

After a discussion Ratti began to share my enthusiasm and we were increasingly drawn to this gigantic tower, which is, incidentally, one of the most difficult and inaccessible (by any route) in the Alps. From the first ascent to the present day, the history of its ascents has mirrored the various phases of Italian rock-climbing development and the South East Ridge was, at that time, its major unsolved problem. We planned to attack in the morning but it was raining heavily so we waited, ready for the first break in the weather.

I remember the first glances we exchanged on the morning of August 15, when the sight of clear skies brought smiles and full agreement. Alvise Andrich and Giovanni Valvassori accompanied us all the way to the base of the substructure. We left at 10.30 and at noon were on the ledge where the face proper starts.

On the first pitch, some 50 metres, we found solid rock and reached a niche before following a short but overhanging crack. The rock there was very crumbly and progress required maximum effort: it is a test of nerves as well as ability, since we had to move terribly carefully. I soon realized that Gervasutti had displayed his usual objectivity in his description of this section, which shared with the Carlesso Route on the South Face. Nevertheless on this part of the route progress was easier because of the pitons left by Carlesso.

I moved to the left and after 30 metres passed a crack ending in an overhang; there I found a providential ledge where Ratti joined me. We recovered the pitons, as was our habit, hanging on the rope and climbing up hand over hand to the next piton.

The face is made up of stratified layers of terraces and ill-defined bands which run across the whole tower. This geological formation gives rise to the ledges and overhangs.

We had been told that it would be possible to reach a point about halfway up the ridge by a traverse line linking Torre Trieste to Castello della Busazza, and thereby reconnoitre and 'prepare' the most treacherous and difficult sections of the route in advance. However, our alpine ethic rendered such tactics unthinkable: they would have diminished the elegance and beauty of the ascent, together with our desire to climb it. Even today I use the same standards in judging an ascent or the outcome of an attempt — excluding, of course, the great walls outside Europe, where different techniques are necessary because of the length of the routes.

I found a cave of sorts in the rock where we stopped. Lush, rosin-scented lilies were plentiful here and they served us well as bedding, especially for Ratti, since it was his first bivouac. The hours spent up there during that soft August evening under the shining moon, with the great tower shooting up above us into the dark, were happy ones because of Ratti's delight in his experience; today those hours seem even more important as he is dead, cut down in the mayhem of war.

In the morning, we started climbing again, up a narrow crevice broken after about 30 metres by a roof which I was able to turn by a crack on the right. Two pitches of overhanging cracks followed until we reached the main ledge crossing the face. The weather was fine, with not a breath of wind, and the rock was hot under the sun's rays; parched throats and thirst tortured us for the rest of the climb. My nose suddenly started to bleed heavily, worrying my friend a great deal, but it finally stopped. This seemed to refresh me; feeling lighter, I started climbing again on a leftward traverse followed by a section of Grade 6, a crack with an overhang at the top.

There followed a number of narrow, overhanging Grade 5 cracks which we climbed free for a full 80 metres to a big terrace. The day drew to a close, but I didn't feel tired as we prepared for the second bivouac on this wall (my fourth in just a few days). There was plenty of room and, but for our thirst, it would have been blissful.

In the morning we started by turning an overhanging roof on its left, then, after a very thin crack, we reached a small ledge and, higher up, a niche. Above was another roof, another ten-metre crack, and finally a platform with a big unstable boulder that made the place very treacherous. At this point there was a hand traverse to the right. I placed a piton, warned my companion and went on, feeling a breath of life in the contact of my fingertips with the rock. A comfortable ledge brought us together again.

The piton we had first placed for a belay had to hold us while, to reach the first holds of the crack above us, I had to stand on Ratti's shoulders. With the advantage of his height, I reached a small step near the spire they call the ''campaniletto' without too much effort.

I had to start placing pitons because the chimney I was following flared out, but after moving up quite a long way I realized it was impossible for me to go any further. Fuming at the loss of time, I retreated and tried to the right, where the wall offered a small step, and started fighting an exposed overhanging crack above a frightening, apparently infinite drop, but I felt sure that the summit was near.

In fact it was three in the afternoon when, after climbing the final chimney, we were on the summit. After fifty hours of climbing (twenty-eight of which were spent on the ridge with the help of sixty pitons), we happily yelled down to our friends that this beautiful route was finally ours . . . and, succumbing to temptation, gulped down the last of the water saved by our enormous and prudent effort.

We rappeled down, our return made even more cheerful when we met Boga's team (he was with Angelo Longoni and Giovanni Giudici, who was nicknamed 'Farfallino' — the Butterfly). They had just completed the difficult Carlesso/Sandri Route on the South Face so we all had good reason to be cheerful. On the final part of the descent we greedily drank from the pools of water left in rock cavities from the storms of days past and then, exhultant, climbed down to the valley.

The ascent of the superb South East Ridge is climbing *par excellence*. It is the true test of human potential, a consistent Grade 5 and 6 route which gives continuous pleasure as the pitons are used more for protection than aid.*

*Recent ascents by British and Commonwealth climbers have confirmed this assessment. The Cassin/Ratti Route is said to be superior in terms of quality, difficulty and line to the adjoining Carlesso/Sandri Route. *Publisher's Note.*

PART TWO

My Alpine Triad

The justifiable pride of Italians in having taken the North Face of the Cima Ovest; the fierce rivalry on the North East Face of Piz Badile, which metamorphosed itself into deep friendship; the keen disappointment of finding out, in Kleine Scheidegg, just before our attack on the North Face of the Eiger that an Austro-German team had beaten us to it, a humiliation soon revenged with the ascent of the Walker Spur: these were the mainsprings of our emotions in our successful attacks on those three faces, which had stubbornly resisted the most qualified of rock climbers.

CHAPTER EIGHT

Cima Ovest

1935: Cima Ovest di Lavaredo (North Face)

In August, 1935, a few days after our return to Lecco from the Civetta holiday, a newspaper reported that a pair of young Bavarian climbers, two of the best of the Kaisergebirge, were camped at the foot of the unclimbed North Face of Cima Ovest waiting for good weather. The news caused great excitement in the Alpine world, especially in Misurina and Cortina, and prompted us not to lose another minute, for we too were keen to attempt this stupendous Dolomite wall.

Helped by our club, Ratti and I, with Mino Rossi immediately took a fast train to Misurina: still euphoric over the Torre Trieste success, we hoped for further glory in claiming the first ascent of the face for our country. Do not tell me that this kind of sentiment runs contrary to the spirit of climbing: would you not want the pleasure of making a first ascent? Would you not throw yourself into a competition with the idea of winning it, especially if your competitors were the best and the prize was of such enormous value? Living in the classic period of Grade 6 climbing, we were confronting its challenge with all the boldness and decisiveness of youth, backed up by serious training.

We left Misurina on foot, loaded up like mules, and were followed for some distance by a wirehaired terrier which, won by Ratti's initial flattery, would not leave us: we were finally forced to yell threats and abuse at him, for we were afraid he would not be able to find his way home. The sky was overcast, the air heavy; dampness was all-pervasive in the fire, the lilies, and the rhododendron bushes.

At the Lavaredo Hut the custodian and the guides soon guessed our ambitions from our equipment, and their guesswork was confirmed by our questions. They asked us what we knew about the North Face of the Cima Ovest, and told us about the various attempts: twenty-seven parties, they said, had been stopped by one terrible overhang, and nobody had managed to reach the great traverse, which itself presented even greater difficulties. It was harder than Grade 6, they said. They mentioned name after name, some prestigious, some that we knew well, whose attempts had been in vain; in 1933 Comici, Mary Varale and Zanutti (the successful Yellow Edge team): Dimai, Carlesso, Demetz; Comici again, climbing the first leg with Zanutti and Del Pianto. I felt my heart beat harder; I longed for action.

The best results were marked out on a card. Above the highest point reached, everything overhangs, and once committed to the traverse there could be no return: the base of the great upper couloirs would have to be reached before there could be any safety at all. From the bottom to the traverse is 200 metres upwards, and 30 outwards; altogether the wall rises for 500 metres, half of which bulges out, yellow and repulsive. Instead of stopping us, all this information merely increased our impatience to start climbing.

But it was already evening, and had started to rain again: the weather had been bad for two days and we felt sure that nobody could be on the face. Meanwhile, at the base of the cliff, Hintermeier and Meindl, awaiting their chance, stood guard over the face from their camp at the end of the moraine, near a beautiful little lake.

"Of course they know what they're up against," the guides had said, "they've done the whole of the first section. . . ."

On August 27, the day after our arrival, we launched our attack, circling round the Croda Hut and past the Forcella of the Col di Mezzo. Dense fog befriended us, hiding us from everybody's eyes, particularly those of our close competitors. We used every trick possible not to be spotted and even made a point of whispering during the last stretch.

The swirling mist parted for a moment to reveal the two Germans outside their tents, peering at the rocks and trying to work out where the sound of hammering was coming from. But they could not spot us, because we were hidden on the first pitch. They even called, but we did not answer. Then the fog thickened again, and we took advantage of it to lower ourselves to the bottom, where Rossi was waiting. Hiding our equipment among the rocks, we returned to the hut in silence. Having seen the ground on which we had to operate, we decided not to lose any time but to attack straight away the next day, August 28.

That night at the hut I tried to mend my climbing boots, whose soles had fallen off: the hut keeper offered to lend me his, since they were the same size and nearly new; I accepted and paid rent for them.

In the early morning the weather promised nothing good, but after breakfast it seemed to want to clear slightly, so we decided to leave. Once again mist favoured us. We neither saw nor heard the two Germans, but recovered the equipment we had hidden the night before and roped up. We had two 50-metre ropes, one knotted sling and about thirty-five pitons (the normal quantity then used for a climb of this class), karabiners and hammers.

Having said goodbye to Rossi at 7.30 a.m. we started up a shallow crack to reach a ledge which we climbed diagonally, bearing to the right, and then found ourselves in the chimney that we had partially climbed the previous day. At one point, the chimney narrowed considerably: we abandoned it and moved to the right to a slightly indented couloir. Then we tried the chimney again. Here the difficulties were sustained until we reached an overhanging roof, but once we had turned this, we found a place a stop.

The mist rose and we were revealed at last: the Germans saw us on the face, while we could watch them below like lost souls, racing in and out of their tent and running to the attack, going up to the right hand of the corner. Instead of getting into the chimney, they went straight up for some 100 metres, trying to use pendulums and climb across diagonally to overtake us. For a while the climb was a real race, but finally we saw them abandoning it and climbing down.

A very exposed leftward traverse of about 15 metres brought us to a 10-metre overhanging crack. After that we moved left for about the same distance. We were faced with a

30-metre wall the wrong side of vertical, very smooth, hostile, holdless, and offering no possibility for pitons or rest.

The difficulties up to Comici's high point were nothing compared to the next 40 metres, which absorbed all our efforts for the next seven hours without a break. It was a ruthless, savage struggle against a wall that seemed determined to use all its natural defences against us. One particular piton took four hours to place as the rock at that point bulged out inexorably. After that prolonged effort my muscles reached the stage of spasm.

I reached the end of the rope, but there was nowhere to stop between Ratti and me, so he climbed for about ten metres up to the first well-placed piton. Making two slings out of the rope, he stood in them and belayed me, hanging in thin air. About a metre above the piton that had been so difficult to place, I tried to place another. The new piton gave me little confidence; I warned Ratti to concentrate and in fact while I was trying to place a third piton, the second came out and I fell about two metres. Luckily the one below held. I tried again and again: three times I fell and climbed up again, shaking and exhausted, but finally my pigheadedness triumphed and I got the piton in.

As I went on the rock continued to present great difficulties, but they were less severe than the section before, and so I reached the horizontal fault which runs across the massive wall to the great couloir. Here I found a small terrace, but it was narrow and slightly sloping. Ratti joined me, and we banged in some more pitons and tied the ropes to form rungs to support our feet.

When I untied myself I noticed that two of the three strands of my rope were completely severed, and a shudder of fear passed right through me. In all the past dangers, the slightest fall could have been fatal. I have never understood exactly how it could have happened. Probably all those little falls that I took while trying to place that difficult piton — which turned out to be the crux of the whole climb — inadvertently rubbed the rope over a sharp edge that cut the strands.

It was the end of August, and the days were short; when

the sun set it was dark immediately. We placed several pitons for security as there was a gaping 200-metre void below us, rendered even more formidable because immediately below our foot-slings the rock was shaped like a balcony in a theatre, jutting out some 30 metres beyond the base.

Just before midnight Rossi called up from below: we reassured him and advised him to return to the hut, but with a rare and praiseworthy sense of hospitality, the Germans had invited him to their tent. Happy to hear this good news, we all had a ridiculous and incomprehensible conversation: all five of us knew only our mother tongue. We wondered how on earth Rossi had managed to get on with them. Later, he told us that the Germans, because of bad weather among other things, had insisted:

"Your friends mad . . . Kaput! You to Lecco alone go!"

After eating we tried to rest, a project with severe limitations. As soon as we fell asleep, the muscles in our legs relaxed and we slid down the ropes which we were hanging on, so bouts of sleep alternated with rude awakenings. The ledge pushed us out and it seemed impossible to resume one's previous comfortable position. At midnight a furious storm swept across the face, but luckily another balcony-like roof above us deflected the heavy downpour out into space, so that in the middle of so much hell, we stayed dry. The temperature had fallen rapidly and the air was frosty.

At dawn the storm blew itself out, leaving a grey and uniform sky. Rossi called up anxiously, asking for news. We were fine; but the face was wet, streaming with water. The temperature grew milder and, throughout the day, the sun broke through to warm and dry the face.

We were poised to attack the famous traverse which is actually a continuation of our ledge. At first the crack-ledge allowed us to move relatively easily to the left, but then it narrowed greatly to become merely a high but shallow, horizontal depression. The lower lip provided footholds, while the uneven upper lip seemed to want to throw one out into the bottomless void: between me and the scree, 250 metres below, there was nothing but air. I have never imagined a space so absolute, and I felt like a spider clinging to the underside of an architrave.

I had to do about 17 metres without stopping. I needed several pitons for protection but they were exhausting to place because of the compactness of the rock: holds were minimal and many were upside down. The wall was pitiless and the enormous strain made me sweat despite the cold rock and frosty air. After six hours I reached the end of the first section of the traverse. From there on the overhang above decreased, so that we could jam our hands into the crack below it.

Ratti joined me, which meant we were past the point of no return.

After another six metres I left the traverse line; the next section could only be solved by using a pendulum to reach a small spur five or six metres below us. Ratti joined me, using just the strength of his arms on a double rope which he retrieved. From the bottom, Rossi, Hintermeier and Meindl followed our every move and yelled encouragement up to us. Utilizing a small ledge I went on for about eight metres to reach a ledge where we could finally rest.

Meanwhile, the weather was deteriorating: swirls of mist rose from below and the mountains were swathed in clouds. In the great couloir, which runs up the middle of the face to the top, there was a gushing stream, while rivulets ran down all over the wall. But stream or no stream we had to reach that couloir because our position was too exposed in the event of another storm.

We went over a roof and traversed diagonally. Abandoning the idea of attempting the couloir because there was too much water, we climbed several overhangs of consistent difficulty to reach a small niche. We thought it dangerous, or should I say, imprudent, to go on because it was late and we could not evaluate the difficulties ahead.

At this point our auxiliary rope, which I have not mentioned, made its first and last contribution. On a spool in his pack, Ratti had 250 metres of cord, one end of which was held by Rossi. As Ratti moved the string unwound, keeping us in constant contact with the base. Because of the overhang of the wall, the string had unwound without snagging; we had brought it in case we needed something from below, like food or equipment, but had not yet used it and it had almost run out. Before letting it go we yelled to Rossi to send us something.

We were appallingly thirsty, longing for some hot tea; instead we got two salt ham sandwiches — the most inappropriate thing imaginable. We ate them anyway and, cursing, threw the useless cord away.

Anchored to the face with pitons, we wriggled into our bivouac sac, where we spent a long and hellish night, interrupted by the crackling lightning and crashing rain which came down in torrents carried by the wind. Dawn could not come soon enough to us, huddled in our niche, clothes stiff with water and frost.

Daybreak: another grey one. Within two hours we had passed the overhanging yellow section that had stopped us the night before and reached the lip of the couloir, where we stopped at a beautiful, heaven-sent cave. Meanwhile, the temperature had dropped. First snow, then whipping hail plastered the face. We crawled into our bivouac sac to wait. A pale sun appeared around 11 a.m., but it was still intensely cold and the whole face was covered with verglas. We reassured our friends by answering their anxious calls.

Ratti and I decided to go on, although it looked as if the verglas were not going to melt, and I cleared the holds with my hammer. We were now in the great couloir that runs right to the top; at first the rock was not so steep but was encrusted in ice. Wearing klettershue, I did my best to move steadily, and ran out the whole rope protected only by a single piton. While I was trying to place another, first my right foot and then my left, slipped. Instinctively I threw myself on the rock, managed to grab a hold and stop myself. Then I banged in a good solid piton.

I was terribly shaken, because a fall at that point would have meant certain tragedy. It had been over in a second and Ratti had no inkling of what had happened: I suggested that he climb up with great care because everything was treacherous.

We moved on to the last section, which was easier despite

the verglas, and by climbing in and out of the couloir we were finally on the summit at three o'clock in the afternoon. We had been on the face for sixty hours, twenty-seven of which were spent climbing, and had used sixty pitons, twenty-five of which were left fixed.

I was indescribably happy, overwhelmed by a flood of strong and profound sensations: the pride of having done an ascent which was and would be to the glory of Italy, and the satisfaction of having succeeded where nobody else had.

At the summit, we found our two German competitors waiting for us, and were moved by their noble and gallant gesture. Later, we became close friends and they were the first to repeat our climb. With Hintermeier's camera, Rossi snapped a souvenir photo.

When we arrived back in Lecco, we were met at the station by the town band; there were speeches, processions, and celebrations . . . we had not expected to be famous.

19 The 1934 Cassin/Frattini/Varallo Route (Grade 6) on the North Spur of Cimone della Bagozza. The crux section is indicated by the obvious right kink in the route at half height.

20, 21 The South and East Faces of Torre Costanza. The routes marked are the Cassin/Pilono/Lazzeri Route (Grade 6) on the left and the Cassin/Varale/Dell'Oro Route (Grade 5).

22 The Nuova Italia group in Misurina in the summer of 1933. Left to right (standing): Alberto Carrera, Giuseppe Castelnuovo, Pierino de Capitani, Mario Dell'Oro (Boga), Gino Ferrari, Ugo Tizzoni, unknown, Riccardo Cassin, Bertta (Group President), coach driver, Antonio Piloni; (kneeling) Aldo de Capitani, Giuseppe Riva (Sora), Vittorio Panzeri, Augusto Corti and Giuseppe Comi.

23 The 1933 Cassin/Vitali/Pozzi Route (Grade 6) on the South Face of Cima Piccolissima.

24 Riccardo Cassin practising artificial climbing on the Corno del Nibbio.

25 A sequence of photographs showing primitive artificial techniques in use during the first ascent of the North Face of Cima Grande. The method was tiring for both leader and second as the double ropes were held alternately

26 The North Face of Monte Civetta with the Comici/Benedetti Route on the left and the Solleder/Lettenbauer Route on the right. The Cassin/Dell'Oro finish to the Comici Route is marked with a broken line.

27 The South East Ridge of Torre Trieste with the Cassin/Ratti Route marked. Cima della Busazza is the dominating peak in the background. The Carlesso/Sandri Route on the tower takes the shadowy walls to the left of the Cassin Route.

28 Joseph Meindl on the great traverse of the North Face of Cima Ovest. This photograph was taken by Hans Hintermeier during the second ascent of the face, a few days after Cassin and Ratti had completed their ascent.

29 Joseph Meindl, Vittorio Ratti, Riccardo Cassin and Hans Hintermeier after the first ascent of Cima Ovest's North Face.

30 The Cassin/Ratti Route on the North Face of Cima Ovest.

31 (left) The North East Face of Piz Badile with the line and positions of the Cassin/Esposito/Ratti/Molteni/Valsecchi Route marked. The broken line marks the Molteni/Valsecchi start.

32 The crux pitch on the North East Face of Piz Badile — the diedre just above the snow patch. This photograph shows Cassin leading during his first repeat of the route in 1952.

34 Piz Badile: the deep chimney/couloir directly above the site of the Second Cassin Bivouac.

35, 36 Gino Esposito (left) and Vittorio Ratti training on Corno del Nibbio before the Piz Badile ascent.

CHAPTER NINE

A Great Climb Marred by Tragedy

1937: Piz Badile (North East Face)

1936 found me working as a factory foreman, and this increased responsibility meant I could not dedicate time to the preparation of important climbs, though I remained active on my home mountains; but on June 28, 1937, after intense training mainly on the spires of the Grignetta, I left Lecco with Gino Esposito and Vittorio Ratti, heading for Val Bregaglia. We wanted to learn about that unfamiliar area and take a look at the famous North East Face of Piz Badile, which at that time was regarded as one of the last great problems of our Alps.

Unfortunately, by the time we got to the Sciora Hut, little was visible because the weather had turned bad. With the chances of its improving being slim, we returned to Lecco, but on the next Sunday we went up there again. We walked to the base of the Badile to pick the spot from which to start, then we climbed for about 200 metres on the North Ridge to study the route better.

This gigantic face is divided into three parts: first, a series of very steep sloping slabs; second, a black couloir swept by frequent stonefall; third, a section crossed diagonally by long chimneys and parallel colours. We were satisfied with our exploration but the menacing sky made us turn back.

As we were leaving the Sciora Hut, the Como climbers, Mario Molteni and Giuseppe Valsecchi, whom we knew as enthusiastic and frequent visitors to the Grigna, arrived. They too had designs on the North East Face. We greeted each other cheerfully despite our being in competition this time. It was the third summer that Molteni had returned to the assault: he showed us his proposed route, the ledge where he had spent the night, the high points of his various attempts, the place where he had fallen the previous year. We had already heard of his epic four-day retreat after that attempt.

Valsecchi and Molteni declined our offer of the keys of the hut, contenting themselves with the planks in the adjoining open shack for economic reasons. They were settling in as we returned to Lecco, and we spent a terrible week wondering whether they were climbing and, if so, how far they had got.

On the night of July 12, we were at the hut again with our friends Giuseppe Comi, Gianni Todeschini, Dante Milani and Piero Nasatti. The Como climbers were still there. The weather was still unsatisfactory, so we decided to wait for it to get better before attacking the face. We spent that evening in the hut laughing: Todeschini turned cook and made a refrigerator outside the hut out of rocks and planks which instantly attracted a large raven that visitors of Val Masino had called 'Gigiat' in memory of a legend still heard on the south side of the Badile. We amused ourselves embroidering the tale.

On Tuesday morning, still intent on becoming familiar with the granite formation, we climbed the North Ridge of the Badile, this time for about 600 metres, and then returned roped up. We were in top physical condition because of our training. On the glacier we found three chamois killed by an avalanche, which provoked an amusing altercation between me, trying to persuade my friends how good the meat was, and them, threatening me with total isolation if I brought it back to the hut: but our dinner consisted of soup and chamois meat, at first resisted but then praised and savoured by all present. These moments enlivened a boring day spent waiting to attack the face. Before going to bed we prepared everything for the next morning.

On Wednesday, July 14, the alarm went off at 2 a.m., but the sky was cloudy: the rain that followed sent us back to our bunks. Later the weather turned fair, so we attacked.

We left at 8 a.m. — the Como climbers had left three hours earlier. This did not worry us because the attack point chosen by Molteni and Valsecchi was about 100 metres to the right of ours and the route we intended to do was the more natural line. At 10 a.m. we were at the foot of the face and its impressive steepness now became fully apparent. It had a sort of massive simplicity yet this was combined with an over-powering, brooding mystery that dominated our thoughts; we shivered, put on our klettershue and started climbing, me first, then Esposito, then Ratti. The weather was splendid.

Once over the bergschrund, we were on the face. The first 100 metres, on a diagonal ledge leading to the right, were not very difficult, and after an hour we overtook the climbers from Como.

We climbed across to a big buttress and circled above it to reach the base of a slabby diedre, which we followed to gain easier-angled rock. The natural route now went up along a diagonal crack to the left. This led to a series of upside-down diedres — steep diagonal grooves with overhanging right walls. This whole section from the top of the first diedre took four or five rope-lengths.

At the end of the first day we stopped to bivouac on a comfortable ledge at the top of the diedres, having explored the face above for another 50 metres. We felt very satisfied with the work we had done. Later Valsecchi and Molteni reached us and bivouacked near us on the same ledge.

At 10 p.m. we answered the light signals coming from our friends in the hut, then crawled into our bivouac sac and waited for dawn. The night was calm, not even cold.

On Thursday morning, at 5 a.m., after breakfast we started climbing again. Molteni proposed joining up as a single team. Perhaps the Como climbers did not feel like starting again alone, given their physical condition, which had probably deteriorated due to their having slept out on planks for ten days on end in poor weather. We were quite disconcerted by Molteni's proposal; a rope team of five on a face like that is not logical, but in the end I could not say no, so I gave in to their request.

"Rope up behind Ratti," I told them, putting Molteni last: he deserved that honour as leader and for his previous attempts.

Our progress, despite our cumbersome new arrangement, was good enough. We climbed up an easy section of the face to gain a snow patch. To the left was central couloir which we climbed up vertically for two difficult pitches; then we moved right under a large overhang.

I was about to tackle the overhang, after an exposed traverse: I had already placed a piton above its protruding lip, but I had not yet clipped in to it, while Esposito was 20 metres below me and Ratti at the same height, but half-way along the traverse (because we were so many, we were moving two at a time); Valsecchi was at the beginning of the traverse and Molteni was coming up inside the diedre chimney, about 15 metres below Valsecchi. Suddenly I heard an explosion, a hissing, and a loud sort of rumbling, and looked up to see a huge boulder detach itself from the North Ridge.

Yelling to Esposito to hold the ropes, I flew under the overhang. At the same moment the giant boulder fell on to the bulge where I had been, exploded into a thousand pieces and then cascaded in its crazy course over the ledge.

For a few moments a cloud of dust prevented us from seeing, and an acrid smell fouled the air; we called to each other anxiously, and fortunately we were all safe and whole, except that a big splinter had narrowly missed Molteni, literally slicing off the rucksack and tumbling its contents out into space. But the accident struck cold terror into us: the sensation of being impotent at the mercy of uncontrollable forces, eroded our security and made us uncertain what to do. Nevertheless, as we talked, our fears subsided and we decided to go on.

I repeated the moves to reach the top of the overhang; looking up, I realised, with a sick feeling, that the spot where my piton had been was now completely pulverised! I kept moving, first up a small couloir, then traversing diagonally for some 20 metres and finally straight up.

Towards evening the climbers from Como, who were perhaps not as fit as we, got very tired so we climbed more slowly. The extreme difficulties continued, giving us not a moment's rest; even the three of us began to feel the strain, but we could not stop: we had to find a bivouac spot before dark.

With an exposed traverse to the left I reached the couloir

running down from the spur. From the Val Bregaglia came swirls of mist and the sky was slowly clouding over. We went on for another 30 metres to the left and by 9 p.m. were on a ledge suitable for a bivouac.

Molteni and Valsecchi were exhausted and we were worried about their condition. Would they make it? When would we get to the top? How many and what kind of difficulties were ahead of us? . . . These thoughts pestered us but we kept them to ourselves, trying to seem fresh, to keep up the morale of the climbers from Como, who were shattered. They had lost all their food, too, so we gave them some. Due to the dense mist it was impossible to signal our friends down in the Sciora Hut.

We had barely settled in to the bivouac when a violent storm blew up: lightning, thunder, and then we were drenched by veritable torrents of water that ran down the couloirs above us. Since our ledge was so narrow we could not move out of the way. At midnight, a strong north wind cleared the clouds and the stars came out, but the night got even colder. The hours were interminable: soaked to the skin, our clothes stiff with cold, our teeth chattering, we waited numbly for dawn.

We warmed up a little with the sunrise and started to climb again. The past night had taken its toll on the Como team and they were quite low. I decided to change order on the rope to: Cassin, Esposito, Molteni, Valsecchi, with Ratti last to help Molteni, who was very tired.

Right from the start of the day the difficulties were extreme, especially since the only way was up a chimney gushing with water. We followed this for several pitches then moved onto slabs on the left. We then returned to the great central couloir with its overhangs and protruberances. We had to push ourselves as fast as we could, because to the north the sky was clouding over.

After two hours of climbing, Molteni and Valsecchi were showing signs of exhaustion: they needed help, which was hard on us but we gave it gladly. We tried to support them in every way and to cheer them up. Around noon it started to rain: we were in the middle of the exposed traverse, across the slabs but we had to go on, given the circumstances, and so reached the central couloir, which continued to chuck water down on us. The rain changed to hail: our faces and hands were lashed by hailstones, while the icy wind froze our soaked arms and legs. Suddenly the hail stopped and it began to snow, plastering the face.

We had to reach the top at all costs: a bivouac on the face in those conditions could be fatal to us all. The Como team had simply given up, both morally and physically: the fight against the face and the bitterly hostile natural elements had completely crushed them. We gave them biscuits and cognac and went on towards the summit. Once we had finally got out of the couloir, the difficulties decreased, but we could not go any faster because of Molteni and Valsecchi. It was still snowing, and visibility was down to a metre, but we felt we had almost done it: it seemed to us that once at the top we would be safe.

At about 4 p.m., we had conquered the face, but the struggle was not yet over. The storm raged more violently than ever: we could barely stand up in the buffeting wind, and the falling snow made everything look the same. Lightning snaked around us, and we were white with ice. Straight away we started the descent to the Gianetti Hut; but about half way we got completely lost. Even the Como team, who knew the area better than we, could not help at all in those conditions. We could barely see, nor stand. And then it was night.

Molteni and Valsecchi were in a serious crisis, and we were terribly worried. Desperately, we searched for a way down but the icy storm whirled round us more and more: the savage elements were gradually defeating the weakest of us. Ratti and Valsecchi were ahead. Esposito and I behind with the collapsing Molteni. We did everything possible to ward off the death that was stalking us: we poured all our cognac between Molteni's lips; I tried to support him when he no longer had the strength to continue, but in vain. Without so much as a moan he sank to the ground, never to rise again.

We stopped for a moment in silence. Our feelings demanded that we take poor Molteni's remains with us and, for a moment, emotion defeated reason: loading him on my shoulders, I tried to go on down, but the effort was superhuman in those uncontrolled elements. On the advice of Esposito, who had stayed to help me, I tucked the body by a boulder, to shelter it a bit from the storm.

We then joined Ratti and Valsecchi, who were unaware of the tragedy. We said nothing to Valsecchi, so as not to upset him too much in his disastrous condition. But when an unexpected difficulty blocked the way and we bunched up, Valsecchi looked for Molteni and, not seeing him, guessed what had happened. Standing near a boulder, he wept silently. Suddenly, he dropped to the ground. In vain we held him up, trying to shake him out of the torpor which had invaded him but he too, without a word, was left lifeless in our arms.

We were all dumbfounded over this second painful loss: we put his body in a safe place and, seeing the impossibility of going on because the night was so dark, we got into our bivouac sac for the third time. Nobody could sleep though. Our thoughts were fixed on our dead friends, only a little way from us, under the snow, and we wondered silently which one of us would be next.

Towards midnight the violence of the storm, which had lasted a good twelve hours, subsided, giving way to an impressive calm. At dawn the sky was clear; the heat of the sun revitalized us. We looked around and 100 metres away recognised the snow field at the foot of the Badile.

We carried Valsecchi's body to the bottom, covered it carefully with his bivouac sac and turned towards the hut. In an hour we were at the Gianetti Hut to tell our painful news and collapsed exhausted on the bunks: we had been on the face for fifty-two hours, climbing for thirty-four, and for twelve hours the storm had lashed us without respite.

Next day we went back up the Badile with the rescue team which had come up from the valley to recover our friends' bodies.

CHAPTER TEN

The Walker Spur

1938: Training in the Bernina Beaten to the Eigerwand
Grandes Jorasses (North Face—Walker Spur)

The 1938 alpine climbing season found me in great shape: I was in serious training with Gino Esposito and Ugo Tizzoni (replacing Ratti, who was doing his military service), for an attempt on the North Wall of the Eiger, one of the few last great problems of the Alps.

In the previous year, my friend Dante Milani and I had visited the Bernese Oberland and, after having studied the wall at length, I thought it possible, even though it presented tremendous difficulties and dangers, especially on the last section, because of continuous rock fall. As I was accustomed to the steep and often overhanging faces of the Dolomites, this gigantic wall seemed to be uncomfortably tilted making it particularly exposed to stonefall.

We trained methodically all winter, stepped it up in the Grigna in spring, and even went to the Disgrazia and Bernina groups, which are more suitable for ice climbing practice. After a forced delay caused by heavy snowfall on our chosen mountain (during those days Sandri and Menti lost their lives*), we left a week ahead of plan because we read in the newspapers on July 21 and 22 that a team of Austrians, followed by a team of Germans, were on the face.

We arrived at Kleine Scheidegg during a fierce storm, to be told that the Germans, Anderl Heckmair and Ludwig Vörg, had caught up and joined forces with the Austrians, Fritz Kasparek and Heinrich Harrer.

Throughout the next day, we joined the others who were waiting with increasing anxiety as the Eiger became plastered with snow and hail.

*Bartolo Sandri and Mario Menti, two experienced Italian climbers, who died during an attempt on the Eigerwand — they fell from near the Difficult Crack, probably having been hit by stonefall during a storm. *Publisher's note.*

A rescue team arrived by plane from Munich: I was struck by German organization! But then, unexpectedly, we learned that the Eiger had been conquered and the successful team were on their way back. As human beings we were, of course, pleased but as climbers and Italians, bitterly disappointed. Due to the conditions on the mountain, where constant avalanches were now sweeping the key sections, we had to give up the idea of making the second ascent.

On the train, during the trip back to Lecco, I thought over my friend Vittorio Varale's suggestion, the climb I had postponed until after the Eiger — a direttissima on the North Face of the Grandes Jorasses, on the Walker Spur. I had often heard about Mt. Blanc, but I had never been there, nor had my friends. So I decided to do it and, on July 30, left Lecco with Tizzoni; Esposito was to follow later with the rest of the equipment.

Guido Rey, head of the Courmayeur guides, gave us an unpromising welcome, when late in the evening we asked at the Guides' Offices for someone to show us the way up to the face. The fee he demanded was ridiculously excessive and we immediately refused to pay it.

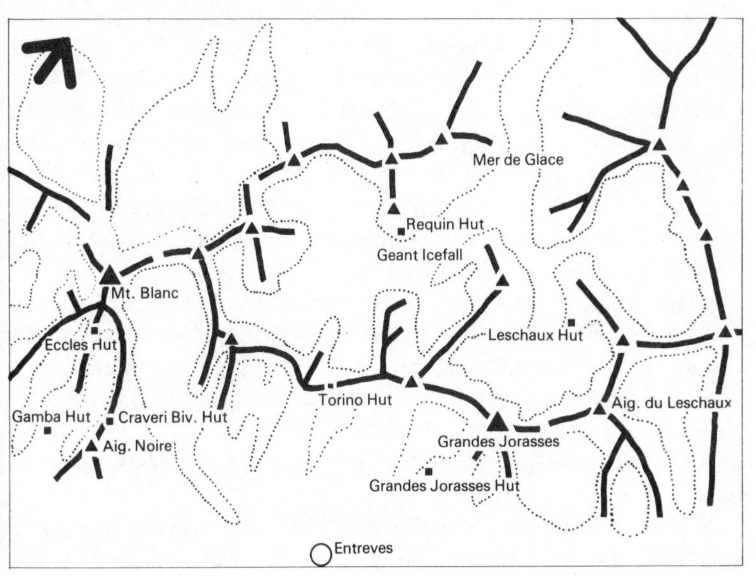

These first impressions were really a bit discouraging, but our will-power was steely: we'd go it alone. Knowing that some Milanese climbers were camped at Entrèves, we hoped to get some precious information from them. We were lucky and later we arrived, loaded with their information and our backpacks, at 1 a.m. at the Mont Frety Hut, where we rested for three hours before continuing to the Torino Hut next morning.

The custodian, the guide Leon Bron, scrutinized us suspiciously and probably thought us two greenhorns: from our questions it must have been clear that we had never set foot on the Col du Geant. Nevertheless, he told us kindly enough the way to the Leschaux Hut.

Roped up, we went from the Col du Geant along the Mer de Glace, which was full of crevasses on the stretch under the Requin Hut; we crossed the place where Ottoz Bron, the great Courmayeur guide, brother of the Torino hutkeeper, had lost his life in the spring; we admired the numerous and superb peaks whose names we didn't even know. At the Requin Hut, the hutkeeper gave us more directions on how to get to the bottom of the face; at first we had to check them off a card but then, as we went bit by bit up towards the Leschaux Hut, the huge serrated ridge of the Grandes Jorasses loomed up, becoming increasingly imposing. Our gaze was drawn to the left, to the highest peak, the Pointe Walker, from which fell a magnificent bastion of rock — the Walker Spur. Even with a heavy snow covering, we could pick out the line of its crest that had been described to us by Mary Varale. It was effectively the most direct line to the highest summit.

After careful observation of the ridge, I worked out the probability of an ascent. The whole of the North Face from the heavily crevassed glacier at its base, up to the summit is a wall, some 1,200 metres high, which would give no respite. The history of attempts to climb this huge wall is a frenetic sequence of names, of episodes with sad endings, and of defeat.

We went back to the Leschaux Hut and, having got some supplies, returned to the glacier to save time and look at the terrain ahead of us more calmly. Frost and loneliness surrounded us, and the atmosphere of ice and rock was totally different from that of the Eiger, which can be seen from the bottom of Grindelwald valley.

The weather seemed to want to turn fair so we decided to mount an attack on the Spur. Hiding the pitons near the hut, we headed back to Entrèves to call Esposito as agreed. At 6 p.m. without having seen a sign of life, we crossed the threshold of the Torino Hut again. Bron was astounded that we had gone up to the Leschaux Hut and beyond. We learned later that while we were going up towards the Col du Geant, Pierre Allain and Jean Leininger had arrived at the Leschaux Hut.

On August 1, we telephoned the Lecco CIA to tell Esposito to come, and awarded ourselves a well-deserved rest in the Entrèves facilities as guests of our friends from Milan. The same day, Allain and Leininger climbed under the great diedre and, hit by falling ice, gave up their attempt. This start had already been partly explored by a team led by Armand Charlet in 1928.

Next evening, August 2, we returned with Esposito to the Torino Hut where Bron, who by now knew us, gave us a warm welcome. On the third day we were at the Leschaux Hut, which was empty: the French climbers had gone, so that we did not know about their attempt, nor they ours.

While Esposito stopped at the hut to mend the paraffin stove and make a delicious spaghetti to demonstrate that his talents extended to cooking as well as climbing, Tizzoni and I returned to the base of the climb to work out where to begin the attack.

Total darkness, which accentuated the cold and silence, enveloped everything when, on the morning of Thursday, August 4, we left the Leschaux Hut to begin our new adventure. Only the first part of the glacier was in good condition: the further we went the more crevassed it became. Nevertheless, the previous day's footprints helped us go quickly and in a couple of hours we reached the bergschrund, which we crossed near the mouth of a couloir of unstable rock, a little to the left of the spur. We went in the order we kept for the entire ascent: Cassin, Esposito, Tizzoni.

We climbed almost the entire couloir, arriving at some smooth slabs where we managed to avoid a small ice fall. We put on our crampons after the first pitches because the slabs were by now totally covered with ice. Then we found some little cut steps, which made us think someone was ahead of us and sent us into paroxysms: and at the base of the famous 75-metre diedre, we found a match and paper scraps.

Taking off my crampons, I attacked the diedre, initially quite briskly, but then, as it got harder, with increasing commitment, until I reached a spacious ledge where my companions joined me. The difficulties were now increasing, but the possibility of placing pitons was minimal. Traversing to the left for three or four metres under an overhang, I was forced to make a very uncomfortable belay with the tips of my boots on one hold, anchored by a piton, to bring up Esposito.

The diedre had now almost disappeared but reappeared higher up as a very steep crack with a smooth, rounded lower lip — and a giddy drop below. Very cautiously, I went on, over a small overhang, to reach the crack and jam my right arm and leg into it. By applying pressure with my left arm and leg, I wriggled along the next ten metres like a snake because the rock, which was completely smooth, tended to push me out.

At the end of this horizontal crack I found another very small crack, this time vertical. I put a piton where the two cracks met and managed to stand up on the lower lip. I went a few metres and without crawling any more, climbed to the right to reach a good ledge, a perfect spot for a rest. Almost all later ascents avoided this difficult part by using the Rebuffat variation on the left, which became evident when a hanging ice-sheet fell, exposing the wall.

Every trace of a previous ascent had disappeared and the moment my companions joined me we cheered up. Several slabs, not too steep but very smooth, then led to the middle of a sort of small amphitheatre, with overhanging walls some ten metres high, covered in verglas. After tackling the left wall, I was confronted by a very steep groove, or chute of ice that had been invisible from below, and suddenly I understood where the stuff that had poured down on us on the slabs had come from.

We put on our crampons again to face this frozen, slightly overhanging chute. I pulled an ice hammer out of my pack to cut steps on its uninviting surface. We climbed straight up for two pitches, then the side of the chute straightened into a vertical wall, so I used one of my special semi-tubular ice pitons which had proved so effective during training. After clipping in, I asked my friends if they were good and firm on their steps, traversed for ten extremely exposed metres and made it back to the rocks. Esposito and Tizzoni joined me; Tizzoni slipped and fell a couple of times while he was retrieving the pitons.

We took off our crampons again and climbed for 50 metres with no great difficulty until we reached a ledge. Traversing right for 15 metres brought us to the base of an impressive diedre.

It was getting dark and, given the time, we considered it sensible to stop: pleased with our progress, we decided to spend the night right there. We were roughly 450 metres above the bergschrund, at the altitude of 3,350 metres. We had a huge meal, because all we had had during the day were some sugar cubes and dried prunes.

The night was cold, raising our hopes for fair weather the next day, but our chances of sleep were wrecked by the deafening cacophony of stonefall in the couloir next to the Walker Spur. I managed to doze off, but we were close together and my friends, disregarding my repeated invitations to rest, abandoned themselves to long conversations and peals of laughter. So, between naps, complaints, stonefall, and my friends' jokes, the night passed.

In the morning, we did a few exercises to loosen up our muscles. Esposito, as he had done the previous night, made tea by melting a little ice on the stove and distributed the rations frugally and impartially, as demanded by the state of our provisions.

Now we had to overcome the gigantic diedre above us, with its difficult overhangs. After careful reconnaissance, I came to the conclusion that the right side was impossible, for it was a single compact slab, completely devoid of even the smallest crack for a piton. So I went up the left, which at first overhung greatly; gaining height slowly and with enormous effort, I got about 50 metres up a rock that bulged and pushed me outwards. Having managed that section, I found myself stalled by a small roof. There was no other way out but straight up over it, using a human pyramid, so I brought Esposito up. Balanced in a desperately precarious position, I managed to place a piton in a tiny crevice after a hard test of my friend's shoulders, an operation throughout which he complained bitterly. Even for me the section demanded continuous and laborious physical strain.

After a short rest I went on climbing and found myself confronted by another bulge in the rock, which blocked the way. But here there was not enough room to bring up my friend and make another pyramid: I had to manage by myself. Luckily, I could place a series of pitons and pull up on them; but getting over this bit took several hours. At this point, Tizzoni signalled that he had seen two people on the glacier coming up towards the spur. We called down to them; they didn't answer so we thought they were strangers, but we learned later that they were Giusto Gervasutti and Arthur Ottoz who, on reaching the rock slabs and finding they had been pre-empted, as on the Croz, changed their route*.

Coming out of the great diedre, we kept on climbing, working on very hard steep ice. We put on our crampons again. I cut ice steps for two complete pitches going slightly leftwards to the bottom of a vertical strip of mixed rock and ice. About a metre's length from it, while I was placing a piton, my hammer bounced back at me and the tip punched a small hole between my nose and right eye. Blood spurted out; when my friends joined me they were alarmed to see a great pool of it reddening the ice at my feet. I stuffed the wound with handfuls of snow and, when it had almost stopped bleeding, Esposito bandaged me up.

*Gervasutti had been forstalled by Peters and Meier in 1936 and had to be content with making the second ascent of the Croz Spur. In his book he refers to an exchange of shouts with Cassin's party in 1938. He also adds an interesting appraisal of Cassin's qualities as a mountaineer, comparing him favourably with the leading German alpinists of the period (*Gervasutti's Climbs*, page 165). *Publisher's note*

"Just like a pirate," said Tizzoni, while I went back to climbing, moving leftwards.

I could see the possibility of going up a narrow chute, but at one point found a considerable obstacle in the form of an enormous roof. I traversed to the right under it along a horizontal crack some 15 metres long but I ran out of rope and shouted to Esposito to follow. He joined me in the middle of the pitch and swung in two etriers attached to one of the few pitons I had been able to place. He managed to put in another for a bit more protection in our precarious position, and belayed me as I went on. But after another ten metres the crack ended, and I could see no possibility of continuing the traverse. I looked up. The roof that blocked our way offered no solution, leaving us to think all our efforts so far had been totally useless. Surely we could not have come so far just to go back?

I decided to force it another way and got Esposito to lower me for about 12 metres; then I did a pendulum and, after several tries, grabbed a good spike. From there I moved delicately across to a small foothold. I looked up again. I had landed under another roof, massive and yellowing, but this one wasn't so bad because I could turn it on the right. After eight more metres I reached a good ledge.

The others followed with some care on account of the delicacy of the climbing. Tizzoni, who was last on the rope had to be particular careful: he was about 15 metres above and to the left of us, and had to make a hard downward traverse with a heavy pack on his back. If he had slipped the consequences would have been very serious, but he didn't and soon the three of us were reunited on the ledge. This crucial section of the climb had taken us about five hours to work out.

All this traversing had led us off the direct line onto the right flank of the spur. Immediately to our right was the huge ice couloir dividing the Walker and Whymper Spurs — a rather inhospitable area, so we now endeavoured to work back to the left to regain the crest of the spur. The route produced ever-increasing difficulties. I went straight up for 30 metres, then found myself involved with two overhanging cracks on the left: I climbed the first, but the second was so smooth that not even a single piton could be placed. I needed more rope; it would have been very unsafe, if not impossible, for Esposito to climb up, so I shouted to him to untie so that I could go on with all the available rope. I realized the danger of climbing without protection in those difficulties but I had no choice.

I climbed down two metres, traversing to the left, and came to a very narrow flat ledge of frozen snow at the mouth of a chute: to my great satisfaction the enormous roof that had forced us to move off to the right was now under me, circumvented. But we were at least 500 metres below the summit, and we would certainly not be able to reach it before nightfall, for it was already 5.30 pm., so our second bivouac would take place right in the middle of the face.

Unfortunately, the weather was deteriorating and in a few minutes snow began to whiten the face. We knew the reputation of this wall and of the Mt. Blanc storms: moreover, we only had a limited number of pitons because Tizzoni had been unable to retrieve many of them in the most difficult sections. We counted them: we had a total of fourteen pitons plus three ice pitons. Would they be enough if we had to retreat?

Tizzoni, meanwhile, was complaining of cold and wanted to reach the ledge where Esposito and I were pondering these considerations. That meant I had to start climbing again because the ledge only had room for two; besides, it was already late afternoon and we would soon have to stop for another bivouac. But where?

I climbed the couloir, which the wet rock made more difficult, and in one rope's length reached the first of the smooth black slabs that follow. After those, I could see, some 80 metres above me, the great grey tower we had spotted from the bottom three days ago and taken as a reference point, because it was two-thirds of the way up the spur. A narrow overhanging crack forced us to make another pyramid and Esposito lent me his shoulders again with good grace, but on a short-term basis. The next bit was difficult but delicious. Ugo begged me to hurry because of the approaching darkness: "Send me a pair of wings then!" I yelled. After about an hour, by which time we couldn't see at all, the three of us were under the Grey Tower on a ledge where we spent the night. Groping in the dark, Ugo came up with a hat full of snow for a good refreshing cup of tea: again we had eaten nothing but sugar cubes all day.

We were 500 metres below the summit. Since space was limited I moved to another little ledge, away from my friends' chattering, so that I might perhaps get more rest. I was almost falling asleep when peals of thunder suddenly rolled through the Chamonix valley: we hoped that the storm would unleash its violence down there and spare our wall.

"That's not for us," Esposito said, and we watched amazed at the wild firework display up the tops of the clouds down there until the sky was as bright as day; it seemed to make the darkness around us more intense.

The next morning the sky was clear enough, but we feared it would not last; we were at 3,700 metres and it should have been much colder. After breakfast — very frugal because we had few provisions left — we started to climb again, at first along a crack which sloped towards the central couloir, and afterwards along a black, overhanging rock wall, moving from right to left to reach the spur shaped at this point, like a donkey's back, above the Grey Tower.

We climbed the corner for several pitches until I saw, 100 metres above, a repulsive yellowish overhang. The only feasible route was on the left, where there was a steep funnel periodically swept by falling ice. Trusting to luck, I headed for it.

I entered a potential death trap in that funnel: at first it was ice, then slowly rock began to predominate, though it was loose and pitons were not safe in it. When we had done about 60 metres, it began to snow and the things falling on us, mostly ice, got more numerous. Finally I found a way out, on the right. After another pitch I found myself under the overhang again, but this time it was only a few metres above and I could go round it to the right, using an enormous granite flake which had come away from the wall a little.

I had to clean the crusty snow from the holds so, naturally, progress was slow. Waiting for Esposito after having climbed a steep chute, I heard noises like hammer blows above me; dismayed, I thought that there must be somebody ahead of us and remembered the party whose footprints we had found the first morning; perhaps they had detoured off the spur. But after a few minutes I realized the noise was nothing but the echo of water drops falling into a little hole from an icicle right in front of me.

Instinctively we now felt the summit to be near, though we could not see it yet. The heavy, clouded sky pressed down on us. Three days of continuous hard fighting with that wall had not tired us and we shot straight up the loose, fractured rock. A gust of wind swept an opening in the mist around us so that on my right I could see the Pointe Whymper, almost at our level. We were almost at the top, roughly 150 metres below it. We went back to the Spur itself and a furious storm suddenly broke.

Surrounded by continuous flashes of lightning, then hail, we could not go on. We put our bivouac sacs on our heads and covered the metal portions of our ice axes. It snowed. But half an hour later everything seemed to calm down and we stubbornly started climbing again; the holds were covered in ice and it got very strenuous.

We had barely entered a steep ice chute when it began to snow again, but we wanted to finish at any cost, which was a hard fight against the relentless, continuous snow. At the height of the storm, about 3 p.m., on Saturday, August 6, we finally set foot on the summit of the Walker — we had won!

We were immediately worried about getting down, especially because none of us had ever been on the summit of the Grandes Jorasses: the only thing we knew was that the least dangerous way began at Pointe Whymper, about a 100 metres away, so we decided to go there. After 150 metres of blind, stormbound descent, I was probing the ground in front of me with my ice axe, when I felt it give way. An ominous rumble followed, and the whole crust collapsed, revealing an enormous crevasse five or six metres wide, on top of which was a snow bridge. I yelled to my companions to hold me but the storm whisked my words away. The rope held, but it was unnecessary: I was standing safe on the upper lip of the crevasse.

Now that the crevasse was completely uncovered, we tried unsuccessfully to go round it: we could not see anything so decided to climb back up and wait for the weather to clear. We went back up to the Spur then, to shelter from the fury of the southerly wind, moved down ten metres on the north side, under the crest, to a small ledge that seemed more protected. While I was placing some pitons for a better belay, I told Tizzoni to look in the rucksack and see how much food we had left. There came a complaint in his Lecco dialect: "Some bloody joke, putting rocks in my sac!" and something whizzed into space. At the time I didn't understand, but remembered immediately afterwards a marvellous green crystal I had found, composed of three faceted stones, each as big as an egg, arranged in a triangle.

"No, Ugo, it's a crystal," I yelled.

"Too late, you should have told me before!"

We made ourselves as comfortable as possible, covering ourselves with our bivouac sacs while the storm raged unabated, snowing and blowing. Night fell: we were standing close to each other with the edges of the bivouac sacs tucked under our feet to keep out the wind, but the gusts of wind were so strong that they got in everywhere anyway, blowing the sacs and threatening to lift us up. Shivering, we felt the fatigue of three days of battle mount up in addition to the torment of hunger and thirst. I massaged Tizzoni's feet, for he was complaining about the initial stages of frostbite. We were anchored to the rock with strong slings or we should have been blown off.

At about 7 a.m., a break in the storm allowed us to see where we were and, exhausted, we put on our crampons and reached the Pointe Whymper. On the descent, because of the mist, we veered too far left; I lost a crampon which was badly adjusted because the strap was frozen. A gust of wind told us we had ended up on the opposite side of the glacier. We decided to go back to the rocks because we thought it dangerous on the steep ice — especially for me with only one crampon.

Fortunately, we met a party of Germans who, besides advising us on the best way down, offered us hot tea and tomatoes and congratulated us on our success. We were astounded, because we had not told them where we had been, but they said that the newspapers had been reporting our climb for three days.

As we descended by the correct route towards the hut (where the Boccalatte Hut now stands) a group of people came to meet us, headed by a strange fellow who was walking through the snow in his stockinged feet, holding a camera in one hand and a bottle of champagne in the other. It was the reporter, Guido Tonella, tipped off by Vittorio Varale, who could not come because of business. Tonella had come to the Leschaux Hut from Geneva and had followed our ascent for the first two days through binoculars, going back and forth between the hut and Montenvers to telephone the news to his paper, and then, crossing the Col du Geant, coming to greet us. With him were tourists and other people who fussed around us and made themselves useful, carrying our rucksacs and gear up to Entrèves.

We had been on the mountain for a total of eighty-two hours, thirty-five of which we spent climbing. We used fifty pitons, half of which were left on the face. We had with us two hemp ropes of ten millimetres, and one of six millimetres both 50 metres long.

CHAPTER ELEVEN

The Ever Powerful Fascination of New Routes

1939-1940: Golem (East Ridge) Campanile Basso (Fehrmann Route) Velo della Madonna Aig. du Leschaux (North Face) Aig. Noire de Peuterey (South Ridge) Mt. Blanc (Innominata Route)

The office work I was doing for ten or twelve hours a day was wearing me down, and in the summer of 1939 I had the impression that I was not in as good shape as the previous year, when I climbed and conquered the Walker Spur with Esposito and Tizzoni.

The winter holidays were, as always, dedicated to skiing, and as soon as the weather allowed, I went back to the rocks of my dear Grignetta to repeat the hardest routes — always a pleasure, besides providing serious and valuable training. When I was fitter, on July 9, Pierino Cattaneo and I made a new route on the East Ridge of Golem, in the Concarena Group. He knew the area and had talked to me about this clean imposing limestone wall that dominates the soft, deep green valley of the Valcamonica at Capo di Ponte.

We left Lecco by car with Franco Galimberti, a close friend, and on the evening of July 8, made the long hike over to the Natone Huts, where the walkers there gave us a warm and friendly welcome. Early next morning, ignoring our slight doubts at the sight of mist crawling up the chimneys, we set out. Galimberti was to follow our progress from the base, alternately watching us and eating gluttonously.

Pierino's objective was an 800-metre rocky spur which ran straight up to the terminal ridge. It was direct and somewhat serious. We made our way through the rocky pastures, to the bottom of the spur, and then roped up to climb a well-defined crack. A difficult and strenuous diedre followed, ending under a roof.

Swinging left, we moved on to the upper part of the ridge, a crest sticking out like the prow of a ship. I had to go round a block by lowering myself on a double rope to a ledge. The climb, an interesting one, gave me great pleasure: serenity and tranquillity alternated with the satisfying sensation of being able to climb again. Climbers should never be worried; careful calculation of the dangers is indispensible, but you must have a clear, calm mind because fear destroys your nerves just as tension destroys your coordination.

Near the top it got easier, but we could not relax yet because the rock was so crumbly. After eleven hours of climbing, with the use of eighteen pitons, we reached the top and enjoyed the panoramic view, where the soft grey of the sky and the mist swirling up the mountain made us feel that it was all an invitation to rest.

In August, during the annual holidays, I went climbing with Professor Enrico Bozzi, first to the Brenta Group where we climbed the Fehrmann route on the Campanile Basso. Then we drove to the Pala Group at San Martino, an area absolutely new to me. We climbed the ridge of the Velo della Madonna then, without returning to Lecco, I crossed the Po Valley to the Val d'Aosta.

There I had an important appointment with Ugo Tizzoni and the Aiguille du Leschaux and I took advantage of the fact that my student climbers were camping in the Val Veni. It was a series of coincidences that brought me to the bottom of the North Face of this pinnacle: a friend had talked to me about it as if it were a problem still to be resolved, and I, not knowing much about it, had started getting interested the previous winter, but with very unpromising results. The photographs promised to me did not arrive, and the CAI's monthly review gave no news of the face; there were only a few strictly uninviting lines in a magazine. Amongst other things, it said the wall "repels any foolish ambition of conquering it."

Punctually at the appointed time on August 12, we met in the well-known square in Courmayeur and that same night, Bozzi, Tizzoni and I reached the Casa dell'Alpinista at

Entrèves on foot. Palumbo welcomed us warmly, looked at all our baggage and guessed something was up. He tried chatting to us: we, despite realizing this was not the best repayment for his superb hospitality, were evasive, simply because we did not want to tell him about something still in the planning stage.

In the early morning we crossed the Val Ferret to the hut dedicated to Cesare Dalmazzo, where I was lucky enough to find Gervasutti, who directed the Turin Alpine school there, and he worked on the hut keeper to accommodate us as comfortably as possible. We had no secrets from Gervasutti; as soon as we were out on the small terrace, we told him why we were there. Once again, we were on his territory. We had already poached the Walker Spur off him, yet he, like a true gentleman, told us all the details of the pinnacle; his were the first precise bits of information we had.

In the afternoon, Tizzoni and I went up the Triolet Glacier for a good look at the face. It was deep in snow: the heavy snowfall and the capricious season made it seem like spring. I studied it meticulously and picked out a possible route. Tizzoni approved the way I pointed out, and we went back to the hut to get the gear ready for the climb.

We left at 3 a.m. the following morning: the cold was intense and the sky moonless but clear. We followed our own footprints in the snow, a precious trail. It was still dark when we reached the bergschrund.

Perched on Tizzoni's shoulders, I grabbed its upper lip, placed an ice piton, and hauled myself up with the help of an ice axe. The ice slope steepened: the runoff from the melting snow had formed channels like bob-sleigh pistes up which we could climb. The snow base was solid: crampons worked well. But Tizzoni got tired of cramponing and wanted me to cut steps; I refused, ignored his grumbling, and went on climbing my way for about an hour and a half.

Little by little, the ice started to give way to rocks. Our reconnaissance proved accurate; as I had seen, the slope of the granite on the first section was not too bad, though a crust of verglas smoothed out the bumps and filled up the holds, taking away any feeling of security. Only later would the sun melt away this treacherous crust to reveal, except in the shadows, good solid rock. These first 150 metres were Grade 4, with some sections Grade 5.

At about 11 a.m. we reached a spike, where we found a sling bleached by the weather. Tizzoni tested it and wrapped it around himself in case he might use it further up. This discovery proved beyond a doubt that, unknown to Gervasutti, there had been a double-roped descent the year before; but nobody had gone past this point and it was bound to get more difficult.

After a short break to satisfy our hunger pangs, I decided to avoid two large overhanging diedres by climbing an exposed ascending traverse on a ledge. After about 25 metres I found a shallow crack bearing left. This was the key to the climb: it was here that the difficulties really began, and I protected myself with a piton. The crack emerged on an ice slope that I chiselled with my hammer; it shattered like glass. Tizzoni, the constant target of this icy downpour, shouted, "Isn't there ever going to be any way for me to defend myself from your climbing methods?"

After the crack we entered a couloir of enormous, detached boulders. At first sight they seemed dangerous, but then we saw that they were set well into the rock. The couloir led to another ledge; on the right the two large diedres continued; we were glad to be in the chimney.

We went straight up a shallow crack that cut through a bulge in the rock. Twenty extremely hard metres forced me to place several pitons, which Tizzoni recovered with great ability. Down to the left we found a diagonal crack, several metres long, that led to a small diedre, which was extremely smooth and overhanging. The only hand hold, and the only piton placements, were offered by a delicate little crack where I had to climb on fingertips and the friction of my rubber soles; I had to resort to semi-tubular ice screws because the crack at some points was too large for ordinary pitons. We battled furiously with these really extreme difficulties but it still took us almost eight hours to do those 100 metres. I then found a hostile bulge of compact rock with all the characteristics of granite and all its disadvantages: not a single bump, not a tiny wrinkle even. I had to commit myself completely, and for the first time I used an etrier, exploiting fully the advantages of aid-climbing on two ropes. The situation was made even more delicate because we had used the entire 25 metres of double rope that tied me to Tizzoni.

I climbed down again and again to recover the karabiners I needed, often in a position of maximum exposure and minimum security, completely entrusted to the last piton. One well-placed piton fortunately allowed me to stop and bring up Tizzoni, now right at the end of the ropes. Beneath me there was nothing but space. Because the overhang was constantly throwing him outward, Tizzoni got tired following me and, at this point, we had to abandon five pitons, which annoyed us because we might need them later. It was already evening and, with a lot of effort, we found a narrow sloping ledge, hanging out in space, where we bivouacked after fixing ropes to two pitons to form a kind of railing. Trussed up like that, we couldn't fall asleep and time seemed unwilling to pass. The night was as black as soot, echoing with the rattle of stonefall. Eventually it grew light. We watched as the sun rose, a sight so beautiful that words, even the most appropriate of them, are totally inadequate, for the state of mind that such a vision stimulates is just too complex. It is not true that climbers do not appreciate the beauty that surrounds them. Very few accounts of climbs include these impressions, preferring to concentrate on the technical details of a route or explanations of how to do one particular section; but not everybody can, nor wants to, reveal those personal, private pleasures to all and sundry.

We were now only 200 metres from the summit so we allowed ourselves a period of relaxation while the early morning sun warmed our limbs. For the first 30 metres of climbing an open diedre confronted us with Grade 5 difficulties. Reaching a small snow-covered ledge, we tried to work out which way to go. We moved to the left to reach the great terminal diedre that finishes slightly to the right of the spire: first, a difficult shelf of compact granite, and then an ice slope. Above these, I moved to the left side of the diedre and, with my hammer, chiselled off the hard crust of ice to uncover the hand holds: the ice shattered and, on its way down, showered over Tizzoni, whose consequent remarks are better left to the imagination.

We thought the hard part was behind us, but we had a nasty shock. It took a good seven hours of effort to finish the last diedre because of its hard, smooth ice and the three overhangs that forced us outwards. I had to use several pitons for protection. When we finally reached the top we were carried away with emotion, happily enjoying the magnificent sight of the great Mt. Blanc massif. But by preference our gaze swung to the Walker Spur. It was a year since we had climbed it. We remembered the happy moments, the tragic hours of the storm: every moment was, and always will be, alive in our hearts and minds.

To complete the route on the 800-metre Leschaux North Face took eighteen hours of climbing and twenty-five pitons. The second half is Grade 6 and often presents difficulties like those on the Walker, but shorter and less sustained.

To the satisfaction of success that day we added the calm and tranquil pleasure of sunshine on a day of particular, limpid clarity. Around 4 p.m. we started our descent, sinking up to our knees in warm rotten snow. At dusk, we were at the CAI's bivouac site, where we quenched our thirst with fresh water from the spring.

Following the steep trail, we reached the bottom of the valley after dark, where our friend Bozzi, who was waiting for us, played a valuable part in keeping us from getting lost. From the Triolet glacier, he had watched us constantly through his binoculars for both days. At Entrèves, Palumbo uncorked champagne: his intuitions about our success had been confirmed.

1940 was not a good season for important climbs. In May I got married, and war swept over almost all of Europe. Even my climbing activity slowed down. My friend Genesio, then president of the CAI in Turin invited me to camp out with his section in Val Veni, where I found my friends from Legnano, Aldo Frattini, Molinato and Rodolfo Varallo. I agreed to climb the South Ridge of Aiguille Noire de Peuterey with the latter. Neither of us was very fit, so we took a lot of time to complete this stupendous route. We were benighted on the descent and forced to bivouac. During the night the weather deteriorated and in the morning we woke up under a blanket of snow ten centimetres deep.

Two days later we decided to go to Mont Blanc to climb the Ridge of the Innominata. Frattini and Molinato joined us but, at the last minute, Varallo backed out because he was not well. The other two friends and I went up to the new Eccles bivouac-hut, where to my surprise and pleasure we found Giusto Gervasutti and Paolo Bollini, intent on trying a route on the Frêney Face of Mt. Blanc.

We went to bed early because Gervasutti and his companion, aware of the difficulties ahead, wanted to leave early, taking advantage of the bright moonlight on the approach. Our route began much nearer the bivouac, so we left much later; we were to pay heavily for this delay because of the terrible conditions and snow at the top of the climb.

On the first section of the climb we made steady progress, whether on ice or rock, but from the second pitch upwards the rock was covered with verglas, which slowed us down. On the ridge the snow cover was inconsistent, and our progress was even slower and more tiring. We sank up to our thighs at certain points, and often we had to crawl to move at all. We alternated leads because it was too cold to stand still and wait for the other, and we were soaked too.

In these conditions the climb grew more oppressive and time-consuming; and the strain we were under made us feel the altitude even more. At nightfall we were still quite a distance from the top, but luckily there was a moon so full we could see as clearly as if it were daytime. Near the top we could hear voices and saw two people climbing in the shade on the south face: Gervasutti and Bollini, just finishing their magnificent Right-Hand Pillar of Frêney. Congratulating them on their superb undertaking, we all continued over the summit.

More accustomed to the altitude than we, they were invaluable help in breaking the trail to the top of Mont Blanc, though they were surprised to find so much snow and the ridge in that condition. Fortunately, as we went down towards the Vallot Hut the snow grew more compact so that we could go quicker.

We found the hut with a lot of snow in it: perhaps someone before us had left a window open. We tried to make ourselves comfortable, made tea on a little spirit stove and drank it gluttonously. I massaged Frattini's limbs — he said he was terribly cold — and we huddled under freezing wet blankets.

In the morning, after fixing up the insides of the hut and cleaning out the snow, we set out for the Gonella Hut and, in the late afternoon, having refreshed ourselves, we reached our campsite.*

*Gervasutti makes no reference to this encounter in his brief but lyrical description of the Frêney Pillar ascent (*Gervasutti's Climbs*, page 176). *Publisher's note*

PART 3

The Sorrows of War, the Hopes of Peace

CHAPTER TWELVE

Fortunes of War

My climbing activities dwindled during the war years. I was not called up for military service because of my work in a factory producing military equipment, and even though opportunities existed to visit the Alps and make new routes, I restricted my activities to the local mountains.

Many local climbers became involved with partisan work. I had signed up with the Committee of Liberation and was also appointed head of the rock-climbing group, which had the task of maintaining contacts between all the mountain partisan groups and those in the cities. I had no hesitation in becoming committed to this work. I detested Nazism and Fascism, which aimed at controlling Europe and denying its people their liberty. I also found the fascists' inhuman persecution of the Jews particularly repugnant.

Italy made peace with the Allies in September 1943, but on the day the armistice was signed, Mussolini set up his Salo Republic, which allied itself to Germany and, with Nazi support, controlled the whole of northern Italy. My country thus found itself divided into two factions and a fierce fratricidal struggle developed in the occupied area, as the allies slowly advanced from the south.

I kept my job, to avoid arousing suspicion, but in the evenings and weekends I spent my time with the irregulars in the mountains, helping them with food and equipment and organising and coordinating the training.

Lecco, because of its geographical position was an important focal point for the partisan organisation and soon became a serious worry to the Nazi commands in Begamo and Milan. They reacted with massive search and reprisal operations. During September and October 1943 they tried to destroy our organisation; houses, barns and refuges were burnt down and hostages were taken. They also used special troops equipped with mortars and artillery.

We were able to continue however, and during the winter months we strengthened our organisation, establishing effective co-ordination between the Liberation Groups in all the main centres. This organisation was very timely as there followed a stepping-up of the racial campaign and we were therefore able to help many Jews, and a number of allied prisoners, to move up into the high valleys and eventually cross the border into Switzerland. These operations, which involved liaison between one region and another, were extremely risky because of their vulnerability to informants.

By 1944 the Lecco group held a privileged position among the partisan groups because of its closeness to Milan. This meant that our group had the responsibility for receiving air drops of arms and supplies. Early in 1945 the Americans sent in a special mission headed by Giancinto Lazzarini, and we were subsequently able to arm and equip all the partisan groups in the area.

In the final months of the war we carried out acts of sabotage to railways and bridges and on April 26 fierce street-fighting swept through Lecco. My great friend and climbing companion, Vittorio Ratti was killed that day during an action in Piazza Garibaldi, and others who died included Angelo Negri and Alfonso Crotti. A day later Italo Casella and Farfallino (the 'little butterfly' — Giovanni Giudici) were also killed in action. This latter incident involved a detachment of the fascist Black Brigade that was moving up from Florence to join Mussolini at Como. We attacked them with 15 men and they took refuge in a house on Corso Martiri on the outskirts of the city. Although they greatly outnumbered us (they had 150 men) they clearly believed we were a much stronger force and signalled that they wished to surrender. I went forward to negotiate and guarantee their safety. Meanwhile on the other side of the house, unknown to me, they had continued firing and killed some of our men including Casella and Giudici — it was a treacherous act as they were already showing a white flag.*

The war ended on May 8 and for a short period, during the

*Cassin was injured in the arm and face during this action. He was subsequently awarded the Cross of Military Valour for his part in the incident. *Publisher's note*

37 Esposito, Cassin and Ratti at the Gianetta Hut after the Badile tragedy.

38 Cassin training on the Corno del Nibbio in 1938.

39 (right) The North Face of the Grandes Jorasses with the Walker Spur profiled on the left and the Central Spur to its right.

40 Cassin, Tizzoni and Esposito — triumphant on their arrival at the Grandes Jorasses Hut after their ascent of the Walker Spur.

41 The North Face of the Grandes Jorasses with the Cassin/Tizzoni/Esposito Route (left) and the Peters/Meier Route marked.

42 Cassin, Tizzoni and Esposito on their return to Entreves.

43 (right) The 1939 Cassin/Tizzoni Route on the North Face of the Aiguille du Leschaux.

44 Cassin in action on a difficult section of the Leschaux climb. This is the only existing pre-war action photo of Cassin on a major first ascent. Note the double rope technique and the haul rope.

45 Cassin, Paolo Bollini, Giusto Gervasutti, Aldo Frattini and Molinato at the Gonella Hut after the ascents of the Innominata Route and the Right-Hand Pillar of Frêney in 1940.

47 (above) Tre Sorelle di Sorapis with (left to right) the Comici/Fabian and Cassin/Butti routes marked.

46 (left) The line of the Cassin/Mauri route on the Torre del Diavolo.

48 Cassin and Carlo Mauri at the Craveri Bivouac Hut prior to an ascent of the Peuterey Ridge.

49 (top right) Cassin, Lionel Terray, Fosco Maraini, Tensing and another.

50 (lower left) Cassin and Anderl Heckmair.

51 Cassin with Alfred Hellepart (hooded) and Claudio Corti (casualty), after the dramatic rescue from the Eigerwand in 1957. Cassin was highly critical of Corti's role in the affair.

52 Cassin poses in front of Gasherbrum IV in 1957. The mountain was subsequently climbed by his expedition.

53 Bepi De Francesch on the difficult mixed ground that typified the final section of the Gasherbrum IV ascent.

54 Gasherbrum IV seen from Camp 2 at the head of the South Gasherbrum Glacier. The route continued up the icefall to gain the snow basin, and then followed the rocky North East Ridge which is profiled on the right.

summer, I worked for the Authorities reorganising Public Security. By September the problem of reorganisation had been resolved, and I resumed my normal occupation.

CHAPTER THIRTEEN

The Post-War Years

1947: Tre Sorelle di Sorapis (North West Face)
Torre del Diavolo (South East Face)

Soon after returning home I was elected President of our section of the CAI in Lecco. This post carried with it the responsibility for organising the reconstruction of alpine huts in our area, many of which has been damaged or destroyed during the war years. With the help of my friends these tasks were started and before long we were able to get back to real mountaineering, first in the Grignetta, then in the Bregaglia, in Val Masino, and generally throughout the mountains of Lombardy.

1946 also marked the birth of a group called *Ragni della Grignetta*. This was a collection of keen young climbers and they asked me to be their leader or patron. These lads were dedicated to hard climbing and in the years to come they were to make their nickname 'Lecco Spiders' famous throughout the world.

During August 1947 I joined the 'Spiders' in their camp in Misurina, and on August 7, with Felice Butti, I made a new route on the main summit of the Tre Sorelle di Sorapis [Three Sisters of Sorapis]. It was in the Sorapis Group that in 1929 Emilio Comici and Gordiano Bruno Fabian added two new routes, the first of which — the North West Face of the Sorella di Mezzo — was of particular importance.

We left Misurina by car, which we left at the Tre Croci Pass, from whence we climbed to the Luzzatti Hut. From the hut we moved leftwards in scree-filled gullies to gain a small glacier. We continued on the hard snow with the aid of sticks which we had brought with us instead of ice axes. In due course we found a strip of yellow rock, where we roped up and prepared to climb, jettisoning our worthy sticks which went skidding down the glacier below.

After two pitches we reached the bottom of a small diedre that leaned out above and gave a beautiful section of Grade 6. I followed its crack for several metres, swung left and reached the base of an overhanging diedre that required the double rope and etriers.

For the next 20 metres we followed a relatively easy chimney, but then even that changed and narrowed into an overhanging crack of Grade 6 again. When Butti joined me, on a ledge covered in large boulders, the great chimney, visible from the smaller glacier, was right ahead of us. We climbed up via some easy rocks to a ledge, just in time to avoid a violent storm, and sheltered on the right of the ledge itself, which was covered by an ample ceiling.

The air cooled until, standing in the dry, we could almost taste its freshness and we took advantage of the prolonged stop to eat and drink. As soon as the weather looked like clearing, we went on towards the summit, reaching it around seven at night after nine hours of climbing. We had used twenty pitons, of which ten remained on the face, and we graded the route 5, with some sections of 6.

The Tre Cime di Lavaredo loomed out of the riotous sunset light, and the shadows deepened the dark green of the pine forest around Lake Misurina.

Bivouacing was not part of our original plan but, because of the storm, we had to wait until the following morning to come down. The descent had its inconveniences, and in the last section we had to use a double rope after losing a lot of time wandering off-route.

Three days later, on August 10, Carlo Mauri and I climbed a beautiful route, Grade 5 with sections of 6, on the South-East Corner of Torre del Diavolo.

I followed the Dülfer chimney for about 20 metres, up to the first wedged rock. From this point, by doing a diagonal traverse, I reached the corner which I climbed by going over an overhang. The rock was compact, and it was Grade 6 climbing. Later, after considerable effort, I managed to place a rather doubtful piton. Once over the overhang, I brought my young apprentice up.

His look and his smile clearly showed what he wanted: from his embarrassed request to lead I got real pleasure, since I knew I could let him do so in complete safety. He went up on the right, then moved back to the corner where he found an overhang that he confronted deftly. I liked watching him. Coming out above the overhang, he moved left for about two metres and reached a small ledge that just allowed him a foothold. I noticed he had stopped because the ropes were no longer moving: I heard him placing a protection piton and yelled encouragement. Then he went straight up until he was under a much more difficult overhang. Shouting a warning, he committed himself to a decisive struggle. He then reached a friendly ledge that allowed me to join him.

I led through, and the difficulties, still considerable, eased a little. A new overhanging section faced me: standing in etriers and helped by Mauri's management of the ropes, I placed a solid piton. When he joined me I finished the climb in one vertical pitch to the summit.

CHAPTER FOURTEEN

My Best Repeat Ascents

1945-1953: Aig. Noire (West Face—Ratti/Vitali) Traverse of the Sciora Group Piz Gemelli (Flatiron) Piz Cengalo (North West Ridge) Piz Badile (North East Face) Monte Disgrazia (North Face) Piz Logoncio (North Face) Cima Ovest (North Face)

As President of our section of the Italian Alpine Club in Lecco from 1945 to 1958, I dedicated myself to life and to the realization of CAI goals with enthusiasm and a feeling of obligation, but in 1958, because of internal disagreements in the club after the unpleasant exchange following a rescue on the Eiger*, I handed in my resignation.

From 1950 to 1965, I was President of the National Commission of Alpine Mountaineering Schools. These years were, therefore, in part controlled by a double responsibility and my holidays were often absorbed by various Alpine courses. But it did not stop me from intense activity in the Pre-Alps, the Alps, and the Dolomites, where I repeated the more important routes.

To repeat a route, especially a classic route, always gives me great satisfaction. To do a route I put up years before makes me relive the most intensely suffered moments on difficult moves. During the torment of the climb, stubbornly struggling to place a difficult piton, these waves of emotion have a profound and valuable impact.

One of my best repeats was on July 17, 1950, when, in the company of Carlo Mauri, I made the fourth ascent† of the West Face of the Aiguille Noire, by the direct route that was added to the face in 1939 by Vittorio Ratti and Gigi Vitali. I also made a number of worthwhile ascents in the Bregaglia and Bernina regions: in July 1950 with Mauri, Felice Aldeghi and Arnaldo Tizzoni, I made the second ascent of the Leh-

*The events following the Corti rescue described in detail in *The White Spider*.

†The second ascent was made by Gaston Rebuffat and Bernard Pierre in 1947, and the third by Walter Bonatti, Andrea Oggioni and Emilio Villa in August, 1949.

mann/Gaiser Route on the North West Ridge of Piz Cengalo; in 1952, Aldeghi and I made a complete ascent of the Flatiron Ridge of Piz Gemelli; finally in 1955, after a number of previous attempts, I succeeded in making a complete traverse of the Sciora group of peaks with Mario Colombo (Snapitus) in one marvellous 14-hour day. In addition to these climbs on rock I was lucky to make an ascent of the North Face of Piz Roseg with Roberto Osio, during which we were overtaken by a hailstorm, but reached the summit as the weather cleared and experienced magnificently clear conditions in the aftermath of the storm.

A particularly memorable repeat ascent for me came in 1956, when, with Roberto Osio, I again climbed my route on Piz Badile. I was delighted to be back in these marvellous surroundings, so familiar to me and so unchanged since 1937, that I reached the Sciora Hut before I realized it. Surrounded by a cirque of extremely difficult peaks, which I had climbed in that period of my alpine career, I gazed once again up and down the arduous spires of the Sciora, across the famous 'Flatiron' of the Gemelli, up to the Cengalo and finally, bemusedly, on the immensity of the Badile.

Then in the summer of 1971, with young 'Spiders', Pino Negri, Mario Conti, and my son, Pierantonio, I did the same route again so I could film the ascent. It was a beautiful day and the sun warmed us. On the approach, I remembered the influence on my character that the conquest of this wall had: it was an episode that filled out my life.

As the route on the Badile unravels it skips over impressive overhangs and offers some bold solutions but during its many repetitions it has certainly been pitoned excessively! And to think that the climb is so beautiful when it is done free! But I didn't let it upset me, everything was so beautiful: the day, the mountain, and my feelings. The roof of the Sciora Hut glinted at us from far below; I stared at it from our bivouac at the small snow field which sits mounted like a gem, smack in the middle of the wall.

We had started rather late because there was a Swiss rescue team and a helicopter rescuing a wounded climber from the face and we didn't want to risk getting hit by stonefall. Because of this delay we had to bivouac halfway up the route, which allowed me to film the sunset and sunrise in all their intriguing magic. The joy of admiring the beauty of nature, coupled with the act of climbing, complemented themselves, transforming me: a prodigious moment. In the mountains you are worth what you are and not what society has made you; what counts is what you have in your soul and your heart, honesty and determination. When I am committed on a wall, what I experience, I experience to the full.

In the morning we resumed our climb. One rope pitch followed another: there was the great diedre, the hardest part of the climb, then the Second Cassin Bivouac, so-called because of the first ascent. Then the most difficult sections were over, but we still had to be careful. The climbing really entertained me: the sheer technique, the knowledge of my capability and experience, and the ability of my young friends, gave me complete confidence, despite the fact that I was no spring chicken, and allowed me to appreciate every tiny element even more.

During the last 200 metres, I thought how terrible they had been for me and my companions in 1937, with the final end looming so close! But now everything had changed, and at the top is the Radaelli Bivouac Hut, established in 1967 by the Lecco Spiders.

That ascent of the Badile, that memory of a young Cassin who, thirty-five years before, conquered the North-East Face, took on a more profound and affecting significance because of one of those odd coincidences of life: my son, who was climbing with me, was the same age that I was then!

For many years I had wanted to repeat the direct route on the North Face of Monte Disgrazia done by Carlo Negri and Fausto Rovelli in 1942. I had climbed up to the Taveggia Bivouac at least five times, but after considering those last 800 metres, had always decided to postpone the attempt until the mountain looked a little better.

Because of their very nature, ice faces don't allow precautionary judgement, and to know if they are feasible or not, you have to climb them. The ideal conditions to climb an ice wall are reached when snowfall has covered the existing ice and the new layer of snow consolidates and hardens, allowing fast climbing.

In July 1957 I had the chance to try it. There were four of us in two ropes, Arnaldo Tizzoni with me, and Carlo Mauri with Oddone Rossetti. When we reached Chiareggio, the weather was not as good as it had been during the previous days: the temperature had risen and the sirocco was blowing. All the same we decided to go to the foot of the climb, just to see.

From the Taveggia Bivouac, reached at midnight, we moved on in the morning and got to the foot of the wall as the sun came up. On the approach we saw footprints on the glacier, but too far left for the central route: these would end up under the great overhanging serac. We learned later that two alpinists from Sondrio had started the ascent but had retreated because of the unfavourable conditions.

Mauri and Rossetti, enticed by those footprints, preferred to climb from there, but Tizzoni and I opted for the original route. After the bergschrund, we climbed a couloir for 200 metres. While we were on pure ice, for the wall at this point was clear of snow, Mauri and Rossetti were on mixed terrain, always under the overhanging serac. At one point, when we were about 300 metres up, I asked Tizzoni to take the lead so that I could film him as he climbed. He had not even climbed a rope's length, and I was holding the camera, when suddenly there was an explosion above, followed by a rumbling. A block of ice had fallen off — I couldn't understand where from, because it was all rock up there — as it fell it shattered upon us in a mass of spinning chunks.

We flattened ourselves against the wall, hanging on by an ice axe, while the shower crashed over us. Tizzoni was hurt by a blow on the knee, but he wouldn't even talk about going back. I took the lead again and got out of the couloir, moving ahead with Mauri and Rossetti level with us but sheltered from falling objects and on good snow, so that they could move faster. But they had their trouble too: Mauri broke a crampon. We climbed the nearly vertical ice wall in three pitches, reached the serac using Mauri's steps, and went on to where they were waiting for us: Mauri could not lead any more with a broken crampon. So our rope took the lead, and I had to cut a lot of steps because the ice was much more compact than below, not only because it was higher, but also because the sky had clouded over and a cold wind had sprung up.

Reaching a small crevasse that cut the face longitudinally, I got over it by placing a semi-tubular ice screw on the upper lip to get to an area of small rocks, both uncomfortable and untrustworthy. We returned by choice on to the ice and I kept cutting steps until we came out on the ridge about 50 metres from the top. Once on top, we returned by the easy route because we had to go to Chiareggio.

From the base to the top took several hours. It is a very interesting climb and the difficulties vary incredibly according to the condition of the snow. In fact, Merendi and Frisia went up two days previously without having to cut steps, while we had to cut steps for three quarters of the face.

Another fine route that I waited for a long time for a chance to climb was the Vinci Route on the Pizzo Ligoncio, a Grade 6 climb that was established in 1938. The face is situated in the savage Val Codera to the east of Chiavenna. In August 1959, I teamed up with Casimiro Ferrari, Antonio Invernizzi and Giulio Milani to make the ascent. We went straight to the base of the smooth wall of Ligoncio, which, seen from the north, from the Val Spassato side, where the climb begins, is an imposing rocky mountain shaped like a pyramid.

The route was very interesting and we even climbed a stretch where we knew a large slab of rock had detached. Near the middle of the climb, we moved with tremendous care, barely daring to breathe, because we were on enormous slabs that had already partly pulled out from the face. We reached the top in one day, even though we had left that morning from the Omio Hut, on the south side.

Perhaps the most interesting of all the routes I repeated in those post-war years, for reasons of nostalgia, was the North

Face of Cima Ovest by the line that Ratti and I had pioneered in such dramatic circumstances in 1935. Twenty-seven years after the first ascent I roped up at the foot of the face with Felice Anghileri while Alessandro Locatelli (Ninotta) and Emilio Valsecchi (Lupetto) made up the second rope.

My mind strayed into memories of the past, my hands retouched those rocks I had once climbed in all the strength of youth. As I climbed, I wondered how on earth I had overcome those difficulties with the little equipment available in those days and with the little time I had. We took a long time on the climb because I had decided to shoot some of it to include in my film *The Lecco Spiders: 25 Years*. After the traverse we bivouacked at the start of the final couloir; we were soaked because of the copious stream that flowed down from the melting snow higher up. Everyone had to suffer a compulsory shower. Only thirst found its just satisfaction.

The following morning, we quickly moved over to a dry couloir on the left and this allowed us to complete the climb very quickly. What a difference from the first climb! At that time everything had been covered in verglas because it had snowed a lot in the night.

In 1972, I did this route again, in one day, with Aldo Anghileri, Pierino Ravà and Giovanni Favetti.

PART 4

Karakoram: Rebuff and Success

CHAPTER FIFTEEN

An Unfair, Bitter Exclusion

1953: The K2 Reconnaissance Expedition

In the spring of 1953 Professor Ardito Desio wrote to tell me he was organizing an expedition to K2*, with the support of the CAI, and asked me if I wanted to join it. I accepted immediately and enthusiastically, for the great peaks of the Himalaya are a powerful attraction to all climbers. My first task was to join the Professor in a preliminary reconnaissance trip up the Baltoro Glacier, to study the logistical problems and work out the route.

On August 18, I left Lecco for Milan, Professor Desio's home town, and thence by train to Rome. The Professor meanwhile went to Rome by 'plane. Next morning we met with the Pakistani Consulate to clear up a few practical problems, and that evening we left by 'plane for Karachi. We had barely arrived when we got news from the local papers about the American Expedition that was attempting K2. We learned that their first attempt had failed but that they wanted to try again. However, the reports said that the expedition members had been severely tested, and the weather had turned bad. Should the Americans succeed, our plans were to try another 8,000 metre peak.

We stayed in Karachi until August 27, busy with Customs formalities, and then left for Rawalpindi. Professor Desio again went by air; I again followed by train. It was a tedious journey of more than 1,300 kilometres. It took 36 hours to cross the great alluvial valley of the Indus, an immense tropical zone of sand which the passing trains whip up into a frenzy: heat, sand that stuck to your skin, and the dreary countryside made for a long trip. Professor Desio was at Rawalpindi station when I arrived, and we went to an hotel

* K2 (28,250ft./8,611 metres), the second highest mountain in the world, situated in the Karakoram Range of the Greater Himalaya, at the head of the Baltoro Glacier system.

where he had booked rooms.

Ata Ullah, a medical colonel who had taken part in the American expedition, was to join us. He confirmed that Charles Houston's expedition had had to abandon its attempt because of storms. Apparently the Americans intended to try again a year later; but now it was our turn, and it seemed that we had already been given verbal approval. On the evening of August 30, there was a reception given in Colonel Ata Ullah's house, with the members of the American expedition. Professor Desio went alone. The Americans, I was told, showed photographs of their route and campsites, and film of the 1939 expedition. On the morning of September 1, Colonel Ata Ullah and I went to the airport to see the Americans off. I took this opportunity to talk at length with Houston and other expedition members about the particulars of the route of their unsuccessful attempt. Meanwhile, the newspapers announced that climbers from various countries had applied for permission to attempt K2 the following year, which obviously alarmed us.

On September 4 we took off for Skardu. The Government official there welcomed us warmly on our arrival, and asked Professor Desio to make a first-hand investigation of the Stak valley, to the right of the Indus, where six months earlier an enormous avalanche had fallen. From the top of Haramosh, it had inundated the head of the Kutiah Valley, forming a new glacier and posing a serious threat. We were to carry out this task before going to the Baltoro. This entailed a radical revision of our plans. I got busy right away, charting a new route over the mountain passes and re-organizing the equipment. On the morning of September 6 we left: first the porters for Dasso, escorted by a policeman, crossed the Indus on a ferry, and then us in the garrison jeep which was to take us down the Indus for about 20 kilometres. We were not to reach Paiju, our original objective at the foot of the Baltoro Glacier, until the evening of the 21st.

The Baltoro Glacier, when we finally reached it, was tiring ground at first, composed of big rocks, through which we were guided by cairns left by the previous expedition. The surface of the glacier was furrowed by medial moraines composed, according to the mountain they came from, of granite, limestone, or slate. We moved diagonally towards the left bank where the scree, being slate, was smaller and easier to walk on. As we went on, the scenery became even more spectacular. On one side of the Baltoro or the other granite walls and spires towered up, formidable in their height, beauty and strength. The most predominant type were pyramids between five and six thousand metres high.

The afternoon of the 22nd, we were at Líligo, and had met the first tributary coming in from the left. We continued along the south flank of the Baltoro among unstable rocks and boulders. Then we climbed the Urdukas promontory, crossing under one face: it was a beautiful place, at an altitude of 4,230 metres and 100 metres above the glacier, which was used by the Duke of Abruzzi in 1909 as a supply camp and by the Duke of Spoleto in 1929 for his base camp. Among the rocks were saxifrage bushes in flower, a contrast to the harsh austerity of the land. We had now climbed 16 kilometres of glacier and we had only seven porters left; we distributed high altitude gear to them. We traversed the Urdukas, from the left side of the moraine, and by walking the entire day of the 24th, climbed up the highest point on the Baltoro.

The weather turned bad and on the afternoon of the 24th it snowed. The porters preferred to shelter under the big groundsheet, designed for gear, instead of their own tents. They undressed completely and slipped under it, lined up next to each other. Their behaviour was strange: they absolutely refused the boiling water from our pot, after having asked us to melt a little snow in an empty meat can. The only thing that they accepted and asked for was medicine. They had unlimited faith in any drug and there was always one of them gesticulating away that he had a headache, stomach ache or altitude sickness. Their endurance of pain was extraordinary, and the effect of medicine on their unaccustomed bodies was immediate and total.

As soon as I woke up on the morning of the 25th, I crawled out of my tent to check the weather: it seemed to want to clear, but all around us was white from a light snow fall. I admired the impressive Mustagh Tower, 7,273 metres high, with its marvellous 3,000 metre spire and, to the south, Masherbrum, 7,281 metres high; here in the Concordia Cirque everything is gigantic: the seracs, the rock and ice walls, the ridges. The glacial valley is dominated on the south by the Mitre (6,237 metres) and on the north by the Crystal (6,275 metres), like two corner pillars from which evolve the two gigantic chains flanking the Baltoro. From the Mitre arises the Vigne Glacier, above which is Chogolisa (7,754 metres), and more distant, at the far end of the Godwin Austen Glacier, the powerful pyramid of K2 (8,611 metres). We were to make our reconnaissance from its base.

Facing us was Gasherbrum IV which, seen from this side, could be the Matterhorn of the Baltoro, while from Concordia it looks like a vertical trapezium of ice and rock glittering in the sun: at that time nobody had even dared to try it. The landscape is so vast that the eye cannot take it all in.

We went along the Godwin Austen Glacier to look at K2 and stopped where the Americans had had their Base Camp: in fact, we found their clothes, oxygen bottles and other things. On the morning of the 27th, we finally left for the reconnaissance with three porters. It took five hours to get from our tents to the Advance Base Camp, going the whole way on the glacier. We even found an American tent still pitched.

We studied the projected route carefully and realized that one shown by Sella in the CAI magazine, and in various other photographs, is the one the Americans followed. We took a lot of photographs of the parts that interested us, but the summit was covered by clouds. We could stay no longer, because the weather was turning bad and it was better to go back in the hope of not losing a day's march. The porters could now move faster because they were mostly unladen, so we covered two days march in one. But we had to get to Urdukas fast, because the porters had already eaten not only the flour for the day we had gained but also the ration for the next day.

It was getting colder, and we tried to hurry despite the

porters' usual objections: they finally gave in. On October 1 we were back at Paiju. We retrieved the food and fuel we had cached for our return and left some for the next expedition, while a very strong cold wind sprang up, whisking the sand into the air, filling our pockets, burning our eyes.

We should have recrossed the Dormordu River by a *jula* bridge, a frighteningly decrepit structure made from woven vines. But the porters refused to use it because of the strong wind and we had to wade the river higher up the valley. Here the torrent divided into two branches: in the first one, the larger, the porters were up to their waists in water. They got all the equipment across and two of them went back to carry Professor Desio over, who, hanging on to one and then the other, crossed without any problem. When it was my turn, only one porter came across and, while we were crossing the second river, he tripped and fell: I went over his head and into the water. Afraid the current would sweep me away, he grabbed my legs so I couldn't get up. I jerked myself free, but after this freezing bath I had to change my clothes from head to toe.

On October 3, we were at Askole where the seven porters who had accompanied us to the Baltoro got the lamb we had promised them as a reward, and made themselves a huge feast.

We now had eighteen more miles to go, but the porters still refused to cross the *jula* bridges over the tributary rivers of the Braldu, so we had to take long, steep and tedious detours up their valleys to find crossing places. We convinced two porters to cross one *jula* with Professor Desio, who had trouble walking, especially downhill, because of a small injury to his knee two days previously.

We reached the liaison officer's home in Skardu after thirty-two days of marching, and were invited in for a meal with the other guests. Preparations for departure were made quickly, but we had to wait three days for the aeroplane to take us back to Rawalpindi, where I was really pleased to see Colonel Ata Ullah again. A few hours later we were on our way back to Karachi, the Professor by air, and I by train. We stayed in Karachi for two days, and on October 16, we flew back to Italy.

After the positive results of our reconnaissance, we began the real preparations. Along with Professor Desio and other directors of the CAI, I was nominated a member of the expedition. So, like everybody else on the K2 Expedition, I had to undergo medical examinations in centres in Milan that specialize in determining physical fitness for such expeditions. They told me my results were not satisfactory. Nor were those of some of the others, amongst whom were Ottoz and Rey, from Courmayeur, and Pala from Macugnagna.

After that, I was invited with Pala to a more specialized and accurate examination at the Rome Air Force Medical Centre. Three medical officers — a colonel, a major and a captain — examined me thoroughly and when all the tests were over the colonel told me that I was in excellent condition and that I could take part in the expedition with complete confidence. My friend, Roberto Osio, who happened to be in Rome at the time, was present at this conversation.

After this oral confirmation, all the dossiers of the medical exams were mailed to the CAI. Obviously pleased with the good news, which put me at ease about my position with the CAI, I went straight to Milan to tell Professor Desio, convinced that the results would please him too. But I could see from his reaction that he was not at all pleased.

In the time between the medical examinations in Milan and Rome, and the committee meetings to organize the expedition, Desio persuaded me to resign from the committee. He said that since only one person was necessary to organize the expedition, there would be no point, since I worked and lived in Lecco, in my wasting precious time. Chabod, an attorney friend of mine, less naïve than me, advised me not to resign, but in good faith I resigned, because I honestly did not see why I should increase the expenses of the expedition if it were not strictly necessary. The committee then declared, in a clearly biased and influenced decision, that the medical examinations from Rome confirmed the Milan results: I was not physically fit. Since I had resigned from the committee, there was nothing I could do about it. The net result was that just over a month before departure my membership of the expedition was annulled — for reasons of bad health, I was told.

Besides being miserable at not being able to participate in the first Italian expedition to the Karakoram, I was bitter at the dishonesty of the way I had been treated. I had spent two months in the Baltoro in the service of Professor Desio and the CAI, doing my best to fix things and reconnoitre a possible climbing route, and abandoning my own business, which I had just started. Then came the growing doubt (since confirmed by fact) that it happened because the head of the expedition, Professor Desio, was afraid that his reputation might be obscured by mine: in fact, when we were on the way from the Baltoro, the journalists, reporters, and mountaineers preferred to talk to me, a climber, rather than to a geologist. Desio, apparently irked by this, had even asked me not to talk to reporters, warning me that this could cause my exclusion from the expedition. He told me to tell the reporters

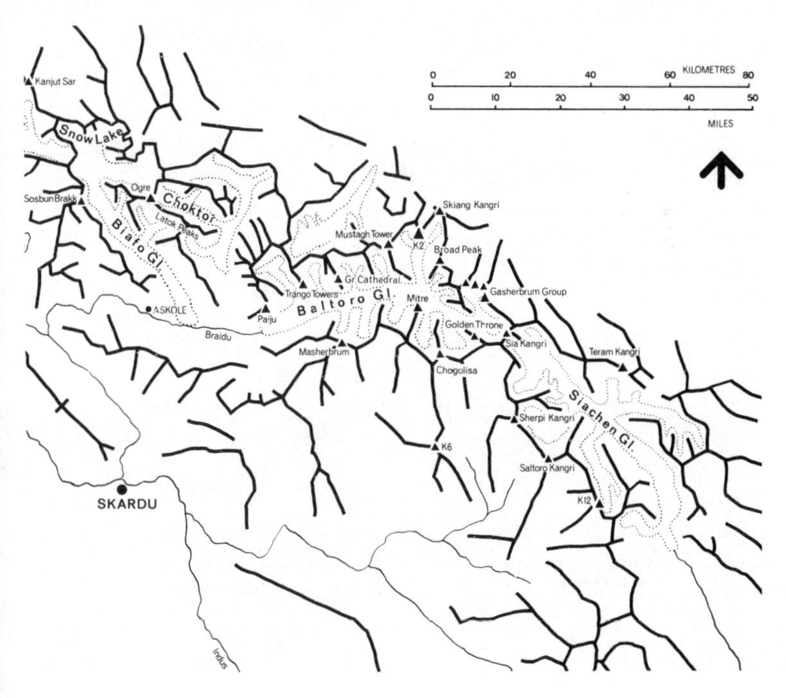

that if they wanted news they should talk only to him.

Nobody would have usurped the credit that Professor Desio deserved for his preparations and qualifications as a scientist. Even if the committee did not want to publicize the real reason for my exclusion, they should still not have based it on the fabrication of 'physical unfitness' — a very serious accusation that was a real shock to me and which affected me for a long time.

I undergo specialized physical examinations often, so there is no need for me to worry, and yet, despite my medical friends' reassurances, every time I start a hard climb, I am assailed by doubts about my health.

To make matters worse, in May 1954, after the departure of the expedition, I broke my ankle during a ski trip and was in a cast for three months. Fortunately, before the end of the summer, my ankle was better and I started climbing again.

To reassure myself that my 'sickness' did not exist, I repeated all the hardest routes on granite and limestone in the pre-alpine ranges.

The expedition, though successful, was not a happy one and was followed by a long dispute between the CAI and Professor Desio. Without commenting on the details of this dispute and the vicissitudes of the expedition, I feel that if I had been present most of the misunderstandings that occurred could have been avoided and, at the same time, I would have had an opportunity of playing a part in a great first ascent*.

* Professor Desio's accounts in *Ascent of K2* and in *The Mountain World, 1954* make no mention of the circumstances surrounding Cassin's departure from the project. Moreover there is only one passing reference to him in the detailed accounts of the Reconnaissance Expedition. The differences in the travel arrangements might be explained by the different financial backing received by each man, Desio being backed by a scientific institution, Cassin by the CAI. The clue to Cassin's demise might lie with Desio's determination that the expedition should be dominated by scientific objectives, or at least that these objectives should not be swamped by the far more glamorous mountaineering possibilities that many were concerned with in the year after the Everest and Nanga Parbat ascents. In his *Mountain World* account, Desio comments: "This project, associating such separated tasks in a single expedition, differed from those of all recent expeditions to the highest peaks in the world, and it awakened perplexity in climbing circles, which maintained that scientific activity would seriously impede the development of mountaineering enterprise." In his book he also mentions the intense interest of the press in the selection of the mountaineering members of the team. These matters may well have led Desio to see Cassin's likely role in the expedition as one that might pose a threat to the scientific objectives.

In the event, with Cassin's departure, the expedition was dominated by the scientists and the mountaineers had to bow to the "very strict Professor Desio" (Bonatti). Nevertheless the organisation and leadership of this very large and disparate enterprise, was good enough for the mountain to be climbed and the scientific programme to be completed; very significant in view of the number of previous failures on K2. *Publisher's note*

CHAPTER SIXTEEN

A Satisfactory Return Match

1957: The first ascent of Gasherbrum IV

After the K2 rebuff, I was tremendously pleased when, in the autumn of 1957, the CAI entrusted me with the leadership of a second Italian expedition to the Karakoram. The CAI had previously asked the Pakistani Government for permission to climb either Gasherbrum I, the last unclimbed 8,000 metre peak of the Baltoro, Chogolisa, or Masherbrum. Fosco Maraini, who was responsible for getting the permit from the Pakistani Embassy in Karachi, told us that unfortunately all these peaks had been assigned. We had to decide on another 7,000 metre peak, and he left the choice to me. My attention had been drawn, during the K2 reconnaissance with Professor Desio in 1953, to Gasherbrum IV. I spoke to Kurt Diemberger, and he agreed that Gasherbum IV is the most beautiful peak of the Baltoro. He added that from Broad Peak to the North and Chogolisa to the South-East, he had seen a possible route. This apart, nobody knew anything about it apart from its obvious technical difficulty. Our permit came through on February 20, and our equipment had to be ready for embarkation on April 10. Funds were limited compared to the K2 expedition, but Toni Gobbi and I got to work and by March 20 practically everything was ready. We spent a week in the Mt. Blanc area testing gear, and then the expedition members went to Monza to pack up the supplies.

On April 30 the expedition, comprising Walter Bonatti, Carlo Mauri, Toni Gobbi, Bepi De Francesch, Giuseppe Oberto, and Donato Zeni, left from Genoa. Fosco Maraini left by air from Rome the same day, to obtain the necessary permits and visas in Karachi, and I followed, also by air on May 10. Having joined up with the expedition on May 12, we left for Rawalpindi two days later in an air-conditioned train. There we met Maraini and our Pakistani escort, Captain Dar.

We now had the frustration of waiting until May 25 for our flight to Skardu. Finally assembled, the expedition, by this time numbering about 450 people, left Skardu at noon on May 30. We reached the Concordia Cirque on the morning of June 15, and elected to use this spot as a shuttle station between Urdukas, on the Baltoro Glacier, where much gear still remained, and our Base Camp beneath Gasherbrum IV. A day was spent in arranging this.

The majority of the porters set off with Gobbi, Bonatti, and Oberto towards Base Camp next morning, the 17th, and I invited Mauri, Zeni and Maraini to go with me to make an excursion to the K2 Base Camp, but they did not want to move. So to fill the free time, I left on skis in the direction of our Base Camp and, after about an hour, met four porters on their way back. They were the ones carrying the flour, and they gave me a note from Gobbi which said that they had not yet reached Base Camp because it was a long march, but that they planned to be there by the end of the day. On the same piece of paper, I wrote a note to my friends who had stayed behind to rest, saying that I would go on for about an hour to study the ground a little more and return later.

Exhilarated, I skied fast, filling my lungs with the crisp air. In moments of solitude I could feel myself open up and enjoy a silent, profound rapport with the natural world, wild and savage: rocks, ice, infinite silence. At the moraine, I took off my skis for lack of snow and walked for a while with the skis on my shoulders. Then, since there was no more snow, I found a safe spot to put them so that I could pick them up on the way back. In two and a half hours I reached the spot where the caravan had stopped for the night. I went on just far enough to see that the moraine continued, which assured me that we would be able to pitch camp in a dry spot.

After a short rest, I decided to go back because I had no food except for a packet of sweets and a little bit of syrup I found in a jar left on the trail by my friends. I was a bit disappointed that I was unable to enjoy the view of the peaks because of the cloud cover: on a perfectly clear day the scenery must be magnificent. I retrieved my skis and went down to the spot where I had found the four porters that morning. The snow had become soft and, even going down, I tired easily because I sank in it. And then it started to snow, and the fresh snow balled up under the skis, making them heavy and sticky. Gradually the snowfall turned into a white-out, but I went on just the same.

At one point I lost my tracks, and then found them again. Without worrying I went on tranquilly, unaware that I was going back on them. The storm was so thick that I could not recognize where I had just been. After passing the spot where I found the porters again, I realized that even though I was making progress, I was not reaching our camp. When I checked my compass, I saw that I was backtracking. I was furious with myself for not having checked my direction before, but fortunately it stopped snowing and I could move more quickly because the snow was now faster to ski on. Yet if I did not hurry more, I would have to make an igloo for the night. I went on in the dark in the hope of seeing the light from the campfire, which would give me a bearing, but I had to be terribly careful because the area was full of crevasses filled with water.

Finally from a rise I saw our tent illuminated in the darkness. I reached my friends at 9.30, after having walked for exactly twelve hours. When I got near the tent I heard them chatting happily and realized that they were not at all worried about my lateness. In fact, they thought I had already reached the other group.

After this the weather was unsettled for several days, and we spent Saturday, the 21st, talking to the porters from Base Camp and their group leaders, who wanted ever-increasing quantities of oxygen and provisions which they were allowed according to Pakistani law. We had to give them so much flour, butter and condensed milk that they could only use half of it and, as a result, we were left with so little that we had to ask them if they would sell us some. Many discussions and delays could have been avoided if we had had an escort with a more flexible attitude. The Americans, for example, were lucky in having a captain who was also a climber and very quick in his decisions, so their expedition was much more efficient.

We finally reached Base Camp on the 23rd, to find Mauri severely depressed because of a very bad burn to his arm, received whilst operating a pressure cooker. Bonatti and Gobbi told me that they had pitched Camp 1 and explored further ahead to where Camp 2 could be sited under the slopes of Gasherbrum III. We had to start the long job of stocking these camps. As soon as our plans had been finalized, we noticed the porters talking to Captain Dar, who came and told me that they were refusing to move unless they got equipment identical to ours. I answered that until we reached Camp 1 there was no need, but that we would, of course, provide those men whom we would use after Camp 1 with sleeping pads, down sleeping bags and down jackets. The porters, however, wanted everything immediately, 'just like Sahib'. I grew so angry I wanted to sack them all, but base camp was too far away and there was too much equipment for us to manage ourselves. The discussion went on until midnight, and at the end we agreed that we would give the extra equipment to the four men who were to go to the high camps.

This type of behaviour — making ever-increasing demands at the most critical moments — created in us a state of nervous tension that must certainly have been damaging; for the struggles and strain we had to undergo, we needed peace and serenity if we were to recoup our energy and acclimatize ourselves to the altitude.

Heavy snowfall, the constant fear of avalanche, and fatigue, conspired to thwart our first attempt upon the summit, but not before Camp 5 had been established at a height of 7,200 metres on the North East Ridge, and Bonatti and Mauri, who had made a rapid recovery, had climbed to within striking distance of the summit. July 19 found us all back at Base Camp.

In fact we all recovered well and in the next few days we reorganized the camp and prepared for the second attempt. It was like being in a shipyard: we made up new rations, ropes and slings, replaced ripped and worn-out clothes, and studied the plan of attack in every minute detail, leaving nothing to chance.

After the first attempt, for which all of us, to differing degrees, blamed fatigue and discouragement, we were now more than ever in hot pursuit of our mountain. We took turns doing the shuttle from Base to Camp 4, taking everything we had decided upon in our highly evolved plan. Communication between the camps was by radio which, besides being useful, was an invaluable comfort and morale-booster because we all felt united and constantly informed.

On the morning of the 27th, we left (Cassin, Mauri, Bonatti, and De Francesch) for Camp 1. After a week of good weather, the sky was overcast. The following day, we covered two stretches, heavily laden, under a burning sun. After a very brief rest at Camp 2, where we found Oberto and Zeni, who for four days had been sorting out provisions and materials, we reached Camp 3, exhausted by the soft snow. On top of that, I had no appetite and could not sleep that night. In fact, when I got up in the morning, my head was spinning and everything seemed to be rocking gently.

The weather was still unsettled but we left anyway. We had two porters and Gobbi, who carried nothing because he had to pack down the trail. I stayed behind Gobbi, but I still found it tiring because my head was spinning viciously. When we reached the col even De Francesch, who had overtaken me, was panting heavily. Toni stopped because he had to go

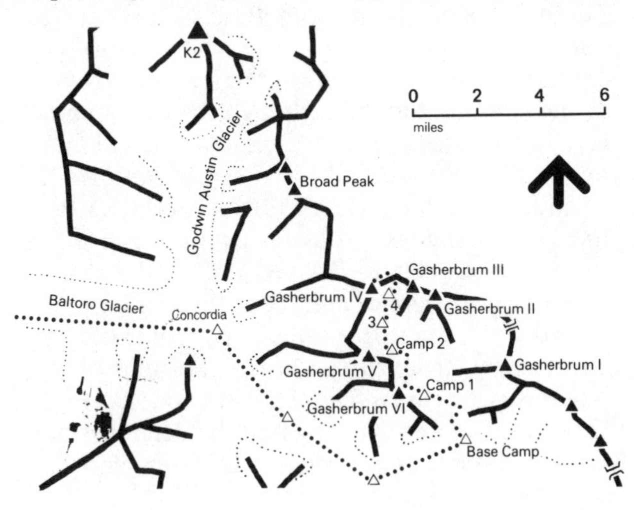

back: he gave me his pack and we went on, in the middle of a raging storm.

We finally reached Camp 4: I was exhausted and felt terrible. I threw myself into the tent after closing De Francesch's properly: he was so worn out he did not even notice that it was filling with snow. I tried to catch my breath, while the force of the storm increased. The right sides of the tents, in the lee of the storm, were completely covered with snow. With a tremendous effort, I got up and made some coffee, hoping it would make me feel better, and gave some to Bepi who, seeing that I was still in pretty bad shape, kindly tended to clearing the snow off my tent too.

During the night there was a real hurricane. At this altitude and in this position, when there is a wind it brings snow even if the sky is clear. I did not close my eyes all night: the whole of the inside of my tent seemed to be spinning continuously. In the morning I got up totally dazed, to hear Bepi moaning that he had had a bad night too. The storm howled constantly and I could hardly uncover even a little of the tent. I could barely swallow anything and, worse still, what went down came back up again. It went on like that almost all day. Towards evening I felt better and even slept a little that night. To think that I had been here for three days and carried three loads to Camp 5 the first time I was here! I suppose my illness was caused by coming up from Base Camp too fast, with subsequent indigestion.

I asked Bepi, who was deeply interested in astronomy, why the weather was still bad even though the moon had changed that day, but he said he didn't understand anything at all, that the weather changed all the time anyway. As if to save face, he added: "Obviously, it's the monsoon season and I'm sure that its influence is felt as far as here, even if weakly."

Every now and then we looked out of the tent to see if Bonatti and Mauri were coming, but they had not arrived by evening and we thought they must have put it off because of the weather. But around ten on the morning of August 1, Bepi caught sight of them arriving with four porters, despite the bad weather: it was snowing and the wind was blowing as much as it had most of the night. They were carrying everything they needed for the second attempt. I was still not feeling well: I knew that I was useless there in my condition and I had better go down to Camp 3 with the porters. This upset Mauri and Bonatti because they were hoping to start the following day, so they suggested that I send up Gobbi and Oberto immediately.

I felt sorry for Zeni because he would far rather have applied himself to climbing than to his speciality as a doctor, and he derived little satisfaction from our demands for explanations about our health. His personality was certainly not best fitted to being a doctor to an expedition of our size. What was needed was a calm, serene, understanding and even paternal person, especially when the inevitable consequences of our efforts at this altitude undermined body and soul. Almost all the porters had problems too. Notwithstanding my definite veto, Zeni left for Camp 4, by himself.

I arranged with the two porters to go down to the lower camps and Base Camp to fetch fuel and food, but on the morning of the 3rd, Taqi came up from Camp 2 with a sack of food and half a cylinder of gas. After two days of rest, I had completely recovered, even though the doctor had told me I was "through".

Towards evening I saw two climbers coming up towards Camp 3. It was Maraini and his porter, Ismael, bringing food and the mail. The last item was a precious commodity, a real boost to the morale at such a delicate moment, and I planned to go to Camp 4 next day to take my companions the news from home.

That evening we had a long talk, an exchange of ideas and hopes about our project which should reach a conclusion in the next few days. I told Fosco I had tried the oxygen and that it worked well, so much so that I intended to leave with Taqi and take oxygen and the mask up to Camp 5. Next morning I climbed quickly, followed by Taqi who, although he was carrying less than I, tired himself out keeping up with me. After fixing the ropes on the icefall, we reached Camp 4 around 10 a.m. A short rest and some food revived us and that afternoon, with quite a load, we reached Camp 5 in great shape. We found only one tent there, for Bonatti, Mauri,

Gobbi and De Francesch had taken the other to the ridge that morning to establish Camp 4, the take-off point for the summit bid.

The weather had been magnificent for three days and we were full of hope that it would stay that way. As far as I was concerned, I felt I had done my bit in bringing the oxygen up, whatever happened. I decided to go down because, to my amazement, the stove to be connected to the propane container was not in the tent. At that altitude one must drink four or five litres of water per day and there was no other way to melt snow. Returning to Camp 4, my legs felt shaky and even Taqi had a headache, doubtless due to the strain and the quick change in altitude.

On the morning of the 5th, I told Oberto and Taqi to go down to Camp 3 to see if there were any porters who could come up with a couple of stoves: Zeni had taken ours with him to Camp 5. But the weather had changed: the summit was surrounded by mist which even the strong wind could not clear away. We prayed that Mauri and Bonatti would be able to manage despite the adverse conditions. I heard voices: it was Toni telling me that they had found the stove and that Zeni was coming down to bring ours back. I went up to find him and met him near the col. He told me that Gobbi was going to take the provisions up to Camp 6 and that he would go too, to replace De Francesch who was suffering from bad conjunctivitis. Considering everything, it would have been better if De Francesch had gone down to Camp 4, for now that I was well and feeling perfectly fit, I could have taken his place.

On the morning of the 6th, I was alone at Camp 4. In order not to remain inactive, I decided to reconnoitre the South East Ridge of Gasherbrum III. After getting into a little chimney, I reached an altitude of 7,350 metres but, aware of my responsibilities as head of the expedition, I ventured no further, deciding to complete the climb later after we had reached our objective, Gasherbrum IV. I left my ice hammer and some pitons for the purpose. Later, while climbing towards Camp 5, I had confirmation that I had actually picked the right route to reach the summit of Gasherbrum

III. A great opportunity lost! Only persistent bad weather deterred me, and Gasherbrum III remained inviolate: it was eventually climbed in August, 1975, by a Polish expedition.

Apart from sampling the south-west side of the mountain, I also took some magnificent photographs of Gasherbrum 5, which is very impressive from that side. I went back via the North East Col of Gasherbrum IV to talk to Gobbi, De Francesch and Zeni, who told me that Mauri and Bonatti were resting for a day, having fixed the next day for the final assault.

Back at Camp 4, Zeni arrived around 7 p.m.: he told me that the ridge was very difficult but that it had been well rigged with fixed ropes. They had not yet reached the white rocks but, weather permitting, they had a good chance of success. Waiting for the outcome of our undertaking gradually became positively agonising: for each of us it became a continuous battle to overcome nervous tension. During my reconnaissance, I had realized how long the ridge was, and that the sloping white rocks were covered in cornices. Towards noon on the 6th, I heard two shouts, which seemed to be coming from the summit: Zeni had the same impression, but the mist and wind prevented the shouted conversation that we had arranged with Gobbi and De Francesch for 7 p.m. And then it started to snow and went on all night.

Early the following morning, I had an exhausting struggle to try to free the tent from snow, but it was hopeless, for wherever I threw the snow, the wind whirled it back into place. I only had to open the tent a bit for everything inside to turn white straight away. Even the pockets of my trousers were full of snow. I was really worried about my friends: I knew they had plenty of food and fuel, but I also knew they were very tired. Had they succeeded before the bad weather? On top of that, the climb down from the ridge to Camp 5 was a hard one, even with good fixed ropes. At least we had plenty of food, as did Gobbi and De Francesch, but there was not much fuel, which is of great importance in getting water — and without that you can't do anything.

Around 3 p.m., I heard voices: I ran out of the tent to see

two figures approaching in the storm. It was Gobbi and De Francesch, who told me that Gasherbrum IV had been conquered for Italy. I rushed towards Mauri and Bonatti, who were following a short distance behind, and embraced them, as moved as they were. We crawled into the tent, for it was impossible to stay outside because the storm was so fierce.

We were overwhelmed by happiness, and talked non-stop, swapping details about the various difficulties. Bonatti and Mauri, wildly excited and grinning cheerfully, looked absolutely exhausted. They told me about De Francesch's fall, which could have changed the best moment of our expedition into a tragedy. Going to congratulate the pair, he had put his foot wrong in the dark and had fallen 50 metres. Only sheer luck had averted a fatality, and the soft snow made a soft landing. Gobbi, who had been with him, had returned to the tent speechless with horror, already convinced of disaster, when there in front of him he saw De Francesch, who had made his way back to camp alone. He couldn't believe his eyes. He thought he was seeing a ghost; only when he heard Oberto laugh was he sure that everything had turned out all right. Gobbi leaped up to hug his friend, whom he thought he had surely lost.

Mauri and Bonatti went on with their story, giving us all the details of the last moments, while we anxiously waited out the raging storm. After a thousand and one vicissitudes, fighting against the weather, they had been confronted by the 'grey tower' at an altitude of 7,350 metres, and had climbed it, overcoming extreme difficulties. The 'third tower' came next, and then the 'last tower'. Finally, on the iced part of the Crest of the Cornices, at 7,750 metres, they had been stopped by bad weather, and had to go down when they were only 200 metres below the top.

On August 4, they passed the previous day's high point and fixed ropes on the 'black tower', which lies above the snow ridge and reaches an altitude of about 7,850 metres. On the 6th, following a jagged ridge, they reached the second highest summit where the granite gives way to limestone, the same limestone which shimmers from way down on the Baltoro; and there was the top!

The summit of Gasherbrum IV is like a five-toothed saw, lashed by winds that bring the clouds up from the saddles flanking K2's pyramid to pour into the Baltoro Basin. The traverse of this five-toothed ridge to the summit was particularly difficult, for the rock offered little placement for pitons and was covered by a treacherous layer of snow which concealed and clogged up the holds. At 12.30 p.m., the summit of Gasherbrum IV was conquered, a shining success for Italian mountaineering. Mauri and Bonatti also said that since the difficulties gradually increased to Grades 4 and 5, they considered the climb among the hardest in the Himalaya (and in those days, without a doubt, it was).

We ate together, and finally, as well as being so happy, could feel calm and relaxed. We spent the night three in each tent while it snowed incessantly. We decided on descent, even if the weather did not improve. With a great effort we reached the icefall, and the whole return trip to base camp was a real torment because of the terrible snow conditions, which made us sink to our knees in some places. The stretch down to Camp 1 was heavily crevassed and a porter fell into one, but fortunately with no serious consequences.

On the 14th we left Base Camp after a hard job getting the porters started: they plundered all the food and gear we were leaving behind, and set off heavily loaded. We reached the Concordia Cirque, but before leaving these mountains we wanted to go to the K2 Base Camp to pay our respects to Puchoz*. The afternoon of the 15th saw us all gathered in front of the tomb of this great mountaineer.

We went back to the Concordia that night, and went on in the dark, extricating ourselves from a maze of crevasses until we found the way out. Next morning, we saw Gasherbrum IV again on the clearest of days, a wild interplay of light and clouds; and in the late afternoon, we arrived at Urdukas. Nature is marvellous: the green in the meadows, the varied shapes and colours of the flowers; it seemed like a dream after months of seeing only moraines, ice and rock.

At Íliligo, I proposed to my companions that we make a reconnaissance of the stupendous Trango Tower, which

*Mario Puchoz, who died during the Italian K2 Expedition in 1954. *Publisher's note*

reared majestically and impressively like a granite campanile: but my idea was rejected because they wanted to go home as soon as possible. In two days we were at Askole, the end of our long journey. As we gradually returned towards normal life, we slowly began to appreciate the immense value offered by prodigal nature. After such a long time of eating more or less purely to survive, there were delicious, delicately sweet apricots which we attacked with almost morbid greed. To the Balti, the seed is of greater interest than the fruit: they extract the almond, toast it, and sell it like that.

We reached kardu on the *zak*; that trip on the cold and turbulent waters of the Shigar River was the last excitement of our adventure.

The Gasherbrum IV ascent showed that, without a doubt, beyond my fifty years of experience and my passion for the mountains, my body was still perfectly responsive and adapted to the discomforts and inevitable complications that arise at high altitudes.

These facts reinforced my regret at being excluded from the K2 Expedition! Apart from anything else, I was younger then. It was even more obvious that the decision reported in the CAI Journal was totally untenable. (Pamphlet 1.2 1954, p. 48):

> The Commission has regretfully had to act upon the unfavourable results of recent clinico-physiological tests on certain well-known candidates, among whom is the climber Riccardo Cassin, who was considered physically unfit for the stress of high altitudes, to the extent that — amongst other things — his life might be in jeopardy.

On my way back to Italy, to my dear Lecco, my thoughts wandered to the days when I used to leave with my friends for Resegone and the Grigna, carrying in my torn pack only a little bread, a water bottle, some dried prunes and the pitons I made myself in the factory. I remembered the Walker Spur too: it was a happy coincidence that it was the same day, August 6, twenty years later, that my pride as a mountaineer, and an Italian, had been rewarded again.

55 The upper pyramid of Gasherbrum IV photographed by Cassin during his solo excursion up the side of Gasherbrum III. The final part of the route followed the ridge on the right.

56 Members of the 1957 Italian Gasherbrum expedition. Left to right: (back row) Captain Dar, Giuseppe Oberto, Dr. Donato Zeni, Walter Bonatti, Toni Gobbi and Fosco Maraini; (front row) Bepi De Francesch, Riccardo Cassin

57 Base Camp at the head of the East Kahiltna Glacier, below the South Face (left) of Mt. McKinley.

58 The South West and South Faces of Mt. McKinley, divided by the Cassin Ridge. The square symbol is the site where Sheldon's 'plane landed.

59 The lower part of the Ridge showing Cassin's route and camps, starting from Base Camp off-picture on the shadowy East Kahiltna Glacier on the right. The left line, taking the full length of a couloir linking the sunny North East Kahiltna Glacier to the ridge, was climbed by a Japanese party during the second ascent. This is now known as the Japanese Couloir and is considered the crux of the route.

61 Annibale Zucchi and Romano Perego on the steep mixed climbing at the top of the initial couloir.

0 (left) The initial couloir of the Cassin route, that led from the East Kahiltna Glacier to the crest of the ridge.

62 Perego and Zucchi move left from the couloir to the aid, move through t[h]
overhang. The true angle of the climbing is indicated by the etrier hanging fro[m]
the overhang to the left of Perego.

63 The Grade 5 overhang on the lower section of the Cassin Ridge.

64 Moving up granite slabs before reaching the Japanese Couloir.

; (left) Approaching
.e Grey Tower above the
anite slabs. Shortly after
is the climbers were
›rced to descend into the
ıpanese Couloir on the
ft.

5 (right) The descent
ıto the Japanese Couloir.
his pitch, which involved
rade 6 difficulties, was
limbed by Canali, Alippi
nd Airoldi in cold and
:ormy conditions.

67 The Japanese Couloir seen from the Western Rib of Mt. McKinley. Cassin's route joins it from the right.

68 (top) Airoldi, Canali and Alippi at Base Camp after their push into the Japanese Couloir.

69 The team: (standing) Romano Perego, Gigi Alippi, Luigi Airoldi, Riccardo Cassin; (kneeling) Annibale Zucchi and Giancarlo (Jack) Canali.

70 Camp 1, situated on a shelf at the top of the Japanese Couloir. This is now the standard camp or bivouac site for parties

71 Moving up to mixed ground above the glacier during the final summit push.

72 The South Face of Mt. McKinley with the upper part of the Cassin Ridge on the left, picked out by the line of shadow.

PART 5

Expeditions

CHAPTER SEVENTEEN

The South Buttress of Mt. McKinley

In 1961, I made my first visit to North America, with the ambitious plan of mounting a bid to climb the South Face of Mt. McKinley. North America is a land which for us Europeans still represents something fabulous, in terms of its history, its men, its level of progress, and its spirit of freedom. Mt. McKinley (20,322ft./6,194 metres), the highest mountain in North America, is located in the remote and mysterious, yet rich and splendid land of Alaska. It was Carlo Mauri who fired the imagination of our CAI section with the idea of the expedition, but a serious skiing accident prevented his participation. With Pietro Meciani's valuable help, we contacted Dr. Bradford Washburn, director of the Museum of Science in Boston. He knew the mountain well, and suggested the magnificent and unclimbed South Face.

The news that a French expedition had the same project in mind compelled us to act fast. The five mountaineers whom I was to lead were chosen. They were young climbing friends whose technical ability and commitment I valued: Giancarlo (Jack) Canali, Gigi Alippi, Romano Perego, Luigino Airoldi, and Annibale Zucchi. As soon as the equipment had been prepared and shipped off, I went on ahead of the other members of the expedition for organizational reasons. Romano Perego and I left from Malpensa on June 5 and we reached Boston after a few hours stopover in New York.

Dr. Washburn showed me his magnificent collection of maps and photographs of Mt. McKinley, and gave us first hand information that immediately clarified the potential difficulties of the face. His hospitality was both cordial and handsome: after dinner, he showed me his stereoscopic pictures of McKinley, which enabled me to assess the steepness of the various facets of the mountain. Our friends were arriving in Anchorage five or six days later, so our host advised us to take advantage of the time by visiting New

York. We wandered through the streets of this immense city, stopping a little confused in the squares, raising our eyes to the impressive walls of its skyscrapers, fascinated by these man-made spires and towers.

On June 9 we reached Anchorage, and were met at the airport by Mr. Dinielli, an Italian resident. In his house we felt the atmosphere of our own distant homes, and again I was touched by the warmth of our reception.

On June 11, I met the intrepid pilot Don Sheldon who was going to fly us to an area near the base of the East Kahiltna Glacier, in his small plane equipped with snow skids. I also contacted Gianni Stocco, a building contractor from home who lived and worked in Anchorage, and enlisted his help to locate our equipment. Both Stocco and Armando Petrecca, an Italian-American from New York, declared themselves passionate climbers and wanted to join our expedition; but I withheld judgment for a couple of days to see what they could do before agreeing to this. By previous agreement, Bob Goodwin, a well-known North American mountaineer, should have joined us, but we had heard no news from him and thought him unable to come. Because of this, I decided to take Stocco and Petrecca with us.

I then flew to Talkeetna, the last small centre of habitation on our journey, in Don Sheldon's plane. Passing over the Mt. McKinley area, I saw close up for the first time, our South Face, a grand and imposing sweep of rock and ice. I returned to Anchorage and the following day the other members of the expedition arrived. The equipment, however, was still in transit. In New York, they told me, they had met my dear old friend, Ernani Faé*, a rock climber and worthy protagonist in our younger years. I promised myself to say hello to him on the way back.

In the days that followed, we managed to transfer the men and equipment, first to Talkeetna, and then to a glacier near the foot of the face, at the spot I had chosen with Dr. Washburn's help. This could be reached with Sheldon's plane and was the closest point to the actual climb. Bob Goodwin,

* A noted Dolomite climber of the thirties whose most important route was the North West Face of Punta Civetta, a virtually free Grade 6 climb of great quality, which he climbed with Alvise Andrich in 1934. The Andrich/Faé is now considered to be one of the finest rock climbs in the Dolomites.

who had just returned from an ascent on Mt. Russell, now joined us, so our group comprised nine members. Sheldon's experience and ability allowed us to transfer everything gradually to the field of operations. Some of the equipment was dropped four kilometres higher up to ease our movements as much as possible and lessen our work. But the spot where Sheldon left us was not quite where we had calculated from the topographic map, for we could not land at the right place because of the snow conditions. Naturally, this created a more difficult situation for us because, from the North-East Kahiltna Glacier where we were, with the equipment deposited four kilometres higher, we had to move to the East Kahiltna. Jack Canali, Gigi Alippi and Bob Goodwin began the work of moving the equipment while Don Sheldon and I returned to Talkeetna, where the others had remained. The

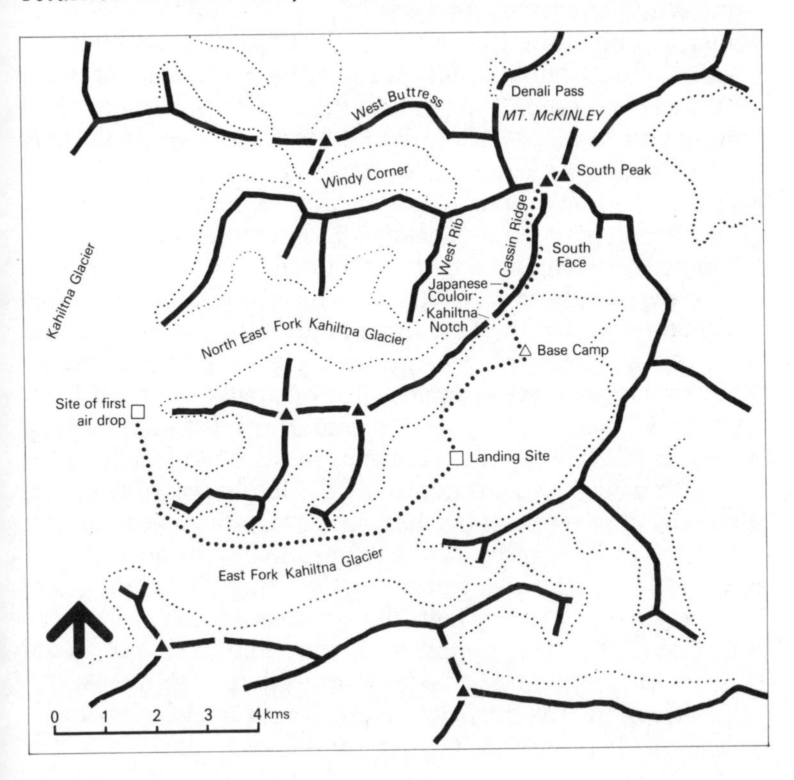

weather was so bad that flying was impossible; we had to wait until the 24th, before Sheldon could both fly and land again.

Preparations at Base Camp were now in their most active phase: provisions, equipment, climbing materials, tents, and fuel had been accumulated there. We worked until 9 p.m. because at that latitude it never really gets dark in summer. In a spirit of self-sacrifice and enthusiasm, each one of us did what he could: we knew that everything now depended on us and only on us. A small, inhabited world came to life, a miraculous contrast to our savage frozen surroundings. Above us loomed McKinley's South Face, which I studied frequently, weighing it up, learning its tiniest secrets.

In these first days before the attack, I quickly became aware that whilst Bob Goodwin was totally competent, Petrecca and Stocco were completely unready for such a hazardous enterprise. Bluntly I tried to convince them to withdraw because they were unprepared physically, technically, and psychologically. It would have been an unforgivable weakness on my part to take them with us. They gave no impression of being able to look after themselves, especially under those particular environmental conditions. On this subject, I should like to stress that a real mountaineer, properly prepared, must always be potentially able to help others when difficulties overcome them.

We were ready to attack the face but the weather remained unfavourable. On the first three days of July it snowed and we were forced to wait: we only managed to reach the landing strip to gather some equipment for our tents at Base Camp. But as well as making our preparations for the thrilling prospect of climbing Mt. McKinley by such a difficult route, we were kept busy by a multitude of simple everyday chores like sweeping tents, shovelling snow, cooking, keeping our personal gear in order, and writing home. In addition, as head of the expedition, I had to act as head of the family and keep everyone's spirits high, be a doctor if necessary, keep the diary, and correspond with our club and our friend Ernani Faè, who had to be kept up to date with the expedition's progress for the newspapers. Cooking also provided a diversion. Pressured by Gigi and Luigino, I cooked a dinner with some fat trout we had caught during our enforced wait in Talkeetna. We had been able to preserve them in our glacial 'refrigerator', and they now provided a spectacular, and morale-boosting feast that was greatly appreciated by everyone.

Goodwin, an excellent fellow, shared a tent with me. It was a pity we didn't understand each other, for we were unable to talk and keep each other company; my companion spent all his free time asleep. With the weather still bad we couldn't start on anything constructive. One development, not unwelcome considering the serious nature of our objective, was that Stocco and Petrecca eventually understood that the difficulties were too much for them and decided to return to Anchorage. On July 4 they descended to the landing strip to wait for Don Sheldon to pick them up while we, at the end of another day spent transporting equipment to Base Camp, converged on the tents, where Airoldi and Goodwin had prepared another good dinner. We discussed our programme for the following days, praying for some decent weather.

At noon on Wednesday July 6, as soon as we saw some sunshine, we decided to attack the big couloir that led up to the foot of the ridge, taking it on the right where there were some exposed rocks. But we had barely reached a small couloir among the broken rocks when it started to snow. Nevertheless, we managed to fix ropes on all the completed section. The evening was spent in the usual conversations and discussions: it was a pity that none of us could sing and draw the others in. On Gasherbrum, Mauri, Bonatti, Gobbi, and Zeni often sang, and nothing seemed better able to raise our spirits.

The weather was beautiful the next day, but a huge dark cloud at the bottom of the valley seemed to be warning us against boldness: we feared that the weather might still be unsettled. We climbed the couloir on the fixed ropes, heavily loaded, passed the previous day's high point, and attacked a new section of rock covered in verglas: Jack was leading and had to work exhaustingly hard to get over it. Gigi then took the lead on a section which was even more difficult. In the meantime, as we expected, it started to snow, but we kept on climbing. Gigi found himself faced with first an overhang which he climbed with a point of aid, then an enormous granite bulge. He told us it was impossible to go any further that way.

I told Perego to cross over to the left, where the chances seemed better, and when he stopped, I joined him to check for myself. We were at a col on the ridge but the mist had meanwhile thickened, and it was late: better to go down and try again next day.

By now I had realised that the couloir we had climbed, was not the one marked on the map by Dr. Washburn, at an altitude of 11,690ft., but an adjacent one which started 200 metres further up the glacier.

Reaching Base Camp, we found Luigino, who had recovered from a slight indisposition, and Goodwin, who had just returned from the landing site with a heavy load of food and a tent. When we began climbing again Goodwin joined us, while Luigino went to the landing site to wait for Sheldon. As it turned out he was too late: Sheldon had dropped the mail and left. We quickly reached the previous day's high point, on the col. The route from here was not obvious. As planned, Annibale, Gigi, Jack and Romano went on, keeping to the left. In the meantime Goodwin and I found a suitable spot, cached a small supply of food and equipment, and returned to Base. This lower section of the ridge was proving to be very difficult and complex. Until we had overcome it and broken out to the snow ridges and the glacier above, it was useless and dangerous to continue climbing all together. It was better to divide ourselves up and alternate attack with rest, taking into consideration the physical condition of each individual climber. On our way down to Base Camp, while the others were trying to force the route to the left, I thought I saw another possibility. Annibale, Romano and I went to check it out, but unfortunately it was not feasible. The South Face of McKinley was presenting all the uncertainty and difficulty I had foreseen as soon as I had set eyes on it. We planned to try again in the place we had previously given up. However, the weather still refused to clear, and it was still snowing. Our 'lilion' equipment was even more precious under those conditions: snow slid off the material, while the ropes did not absorb moisture and so did not freeze. Once again we went down to Base Camp without any noticeable progress.

On the morning of July 8, Jack Canali, Gigi Alippi and Luigino Airoldi were back on the face again and managed to reach a diedre to the left of a prominent rock prow with some Grade 4 and 5 climbing. The diedre was out of the question, being very steep, but they finally saw a solution to the problem: it was possible to climb down into a steep couloir which led directly to a col behind the obvious tower on the ridge above, just below the sharp snow crest that led directly to the small glacier halfway up the ridge. This could be seen clearly even on the topographic map which Dr. Washburn had kindly given us. First they rappelled down, crossed the couloir, which was vertical at that point, then climbed up some icy rifts and short walls to rejoin the couloir above the steep section. Suddenly, thanks to a brief clearing in the sky — doubly lucky since it was still snowing — they could see above the new col to the end of the big couloir and, though they considered the difficulties not less than Grade 4, realized they could reach it.

Next day Jack and Gigi were climbing again, for Annibale had slight conjunctivitis and Romano a mild infection on his hands. Goodwin joined them, jumping enthusiastically at my suggestion. I had to stay at Base Camp to finish several letters and reorganize the film shot in the previous days.

That night a violent wind made us fear for our tents: the sun finally appeared on the horizon, but at the bottom of the valley were the usual clouds symptomatic of unstable weather. Nevertheless, my three companions left at 7 a.m. The wind howled on while I was finishing the correspondence, and even increased. By 5 p.m. it was so strong that it almost flattened the Pamir tent. Inside the tents the continuous flapping gave the impression of a deafening barrage of machine gun fire. I went out for a moment to check the food tent, and a gust of wind almost knocked me over. But as soon as the wind died down, it started to snow heavily again. I was worried about the boys being on the mountain in such terrible conditions and kept nipping out to peer at the first couloir, straining my ears to catch the slightest noise that might herald their arrival. Around 9.30 p.m., to my great relief, all three of them returned, completely encrusted in ice.

The following morning I went up with Annibale Zucchi and Luigino Airoldi, the latter leading. Annibale was carrying the Pamir tent to pitch at Camp 1. Following what had become a normal pattern, I was completely preoccupied with filming and taking photographs. After climbing the fixed ropes we gained the ridge where we found a flat place under the large granite tower, where I thought of pitching Camp 1. We went on to see if it were possible to reach the snow crest I mentioned before. Luigino tried first, but unsuccessfully and on my advice Annibale tried again, keeping more to the right where I thought I had seen a couloir. Committing himself to a traverse on thick ice, he reached its base; I followed immediately, and he went on to attack the couloir, which turned out to be quite difficult due to a layer of fresh snow; he had to use a number of pitons on it. After 40 metres, he stopped, telling me he could only see ice and snow.

When I joined him the situation was not clear to me either. Annibale climbed on towards the crest: the steep face was covered knee-deep with a soft blanket of snow. I barely dared breathe, feeling that everything might crumble at a moment's notice. But once we had reached the crest, we couldn't see the glacier for the thick mist. It seemed to be clearing slightly to the north, which prompted us to wait, but it was late and Luigino, who had been waiting in the freezing couloir for almost an hour, was calling us. We arranged all the gear brought up by us and our companions the day before under the grey tower, at the place where we wanted to pitch Camp 1, and then went down the fixed ropes. It seemed a never ending descent, and we finally reached Base Camp around midnight. I immediately gave instructions to Romano Perego, Jack Canali and Gigi Alippi, who were to climb next morning, alternating leads: they had to organize Camp 1, on the second col, pitch the tent and study the crest formation carefully to work out the best way to reach the glacier.

On the 13th, all six of us were busy: Perego, Canali and

Alippi left from Camp 1 as previously arranged, while Annibale Zucchi, Luigino Airoldi and I followed, after a rest, with heavy loads to refurbish Camp 1. Just before we went back down, Jack, Gigi, and Romano returned with the results of their reconnaissance: the crest was about one kilometre long, and composed entirely of floury unstable snow, under which they could feel a thick sheet of ice. They told me that they had reached the wall of the first bergschrund of the glacier, below which they had pitched a tent for Camp 2.

While Romano came down to Base Camp with us, Gigi and Jack stayed, intending to supply Camp 2, and sleep up there, so as to be ready to attempt the face above the glacier. Meanwhile, Zucchi and Perego were climbing up to Camp 1 with all the gear they needed to go on up to join the others.

Luigino and I on the other hand went down to the landing strip on the 14th to collect the mail Sheldon had left. We saw several distinct marks that we thought were those left by the aeroplane, but when we arrived we found it was Goodwin, who had left Base Camp a few days earlier because his vacation was over and he had to return to work. Sheldon had not yet arrived, and the 'landing strip' that had deceived us was a bunch of little flags Bob had placed to show him the landing site in case of poor visibility. We gave Bob our mail, and left him with profound regret that the pressure of work would not allow him to go on with us.

It was a superb day, and with my binoculars I could see every detail of the South Face, its sweep of ice alternating with enormous overhanging walls, crevasses, and protruding diedres. I carefully followed the projected route that separated us from the summit and at one point I could clearly see Jack and Gigi climbing the first bergschrund of the hanging glacier and going towards the centre of the spur, keeping on its right. From our point of view, it looked more logical to climb the ice couloir on the left to avoid some dangerous sections.

We were now entering the most committing phase of the expedition, that preceding the final attack. I concentrated on studying the plan of action in great detail so as to create conditions that would guarantee our success. So far the rhythm of work we had adopted allowed us all to give our maximum output with the possibility of recuperating our energies afterwards by taking turns resting.

Thus, while Luigino and I got ready to go to Camp 1 the day after we had been to the landing strip, Annibale and Romano were climbing the crest towards Camp 2. Once at the hanging glacier, they made for the chimney climbed by Jack and Gigi who, meanwhile, were returning to Base Camp.

Annibale and Romano continued climbing an icy diedre with Grade 5 difficulties and, at an altitude of 5,200 metres found a suitable site for Camp 3; they then returned to sleep at Camp 2, while Luigino and I reached Camp 1 with the high altitude equipment and the usual provisions, including a Pamir tent. At the beginning of the second couloir, where there were fixed etriers, we met Gigi and Jack heading towards Base Camp for their rest.

On the following morning, the 16th, while we were climbing to Camp 2, we ran across Annibale and Romano, whom I asked to go down to the first col for the food and gear we had left in various improvised caches, and take everything to Camp 1: we were to take the Pamir tent to Camp 2 and then try to reach Camp 3 with the Nepal tents. But the weather turned foul and when we reached Camp 2 it was snowing. The snow fell ceaselessly all night, which made us postpone any attempt. Meanwhile, Jack and Gigi had reached our two other companions at Camp 1 and bivouacked with them. Next morning it was still snowing and given the persistent bad weather Luigino and I decided to go down and join the others at Camp 1. Forced to rest, the boys passed the time chattering in their characteristic Lecco dialect: I preferred to lie down in another tent after drinking a mug of milk. But I could not sleep for the thought of this enforced inactivity, while there were so many problems to solve higher up. In the late afternoon, the sky cleared and we all set out enthusiastically for Camp 2: we decided to head for Camp 3, if at all possible, in two ropes of three, the next day.

In the morning, we realized this plan, and half way up the hanging glacier, heard Sheldon's aeroplane: in fact, we watched him manoeuvring to land and take Goodwin back to work. Then he was in the air again, making some acrobatic turns trying to say hello to us. We went on to the highest point reached by Jack and Gigi, passed it, and reached the place where we intended to pitch Camp 3, at the site identified by Annibale and Romano. In an icy wind, buffetted by continuous blasts, we flattened a small terrace and pitched the two tents of Camp 3 at 5,200 metres. The cold was intense and we felt really confined in the tiny tents, but we were so tired that we slept anyway. It snowed during the night, but in the morning the weather seemed favourable.

We prepared the necessary gear for the final assault and all six of us left, divided into two ropes. The first team comprised Zucchi, Perego and Airoldi; the second, Alippi, Canali and me. Our plan was to attempt to reach the summit, and then go back without stopping to Camp 3. I was aware of the risks but, because of the bad weather, could see no other way. Each of us knew the strains, sacrifices and commitments we were to take on this decisive day. The boys were truly magnificent in their complete dedication to the ascent, though a certain nervous tension showed on their faces. As a matter of fact, they were all, except for Canali, on their first expedition outside Europe.

We climbed straight up the spur, to the last outcrop of rock, took a brief rest and conferred on the route: before us everything was difficult and deceptive. I proposed trying on the left, where in fact we found the route leading to the snow and ice couloir which ended under the summit rocks. We were delighted to have found the key, but we had to fight very hard against the technical difficulties and the weather. The snow was succeeded by a tremendous wind from the south-east, which made it impossible to continue along the ridge, where the ideal route lay. The temperature was savage, the icy spindrift whipping our faces. In these conditions I could not take movies or photographs, but we continued to the bottom of the rocks on the last section. The altitude made itself felt here and the climb became extremely tiring, the more so because of the particular types of ground we were covering: now rock-hard ice, now powdery snow alternating with a frozen crust that often gave way under our feet, giving us a sensation of continual instability. It was delicately poised: our mountaineering skills now demanded an equally important contribution from the will to survive. Even the summit rocks presented serious difficulties: we were tired and completely numb with cold, for the temperature was around 30-35° Centigrade below zero.

Suddenly, unexpectedly, we heard the roar of a reconnaissance plane which circled above us two or three times at close range, seeming to want to comfort us in our weariness, which had become unbearable at times. Our stiff boots seemed to have solidified with our feet: Jack, in particular, complained of cold feet. But our goal was near and at 11 p.m., on July 19, we were all on top of Mt. McKinley!

It was almost dark and it was dangerous not to wear gloves, but I took two pictures anyway with Gigi's camera, almost sure that they wouldn't come out. But at least one picture, admittedly not perfectly clear, was to record that we had reached the summit.

We tied to an ice screw little flags, pulled laboriously out of our packs. The wind blew them together, uniting the colours of Italy, the United States, Alaska, Lecco, and our Spiders: it looked like an invitation to the brotherhood of nations. We hugged each other emotionally, barely able to speak. Each of us spent these moments in our private, personal thoughts. Faces glowed with that particular radiant smile that comes right from the heart. Ours was a beautiful success for Lecco and for Italian alpinism!

The boys, wanting to surprise me, had brought a little statue of St. Nicholas, patron of our city, to leave on the summit. We had to return immediately: the cold was extreme and only when we were safe would we be fully able to appreciate our achievement.

As soon as we were under the summit rocks Jack complained of nausea. At first, I jokingly asked him what he wanted to vomit: we had been moving for 17 hours and had eaten only a can of fruit and syrup in the afternoon. But when we reached the couloir, which was quite steep, I heard a sound beside me, and saw Jack falling towards the valley.

Belaying with my ice axe, I managed to stop him. My dear friend, who had generously given his all in the interests of our success, was racked by continuous vomiting. I was really worried about his condition and, to watch him in the most difficult sections, I went last on the rope and stayed near him during the descent: he slipped several times but fortunately I always managed to hold him. When we reached the traverse, we abandoned the now useless pitons and karabiners. The descent was particularly painful for Jack, who, even though he seemed a bit better, complained all the time that his feet were terribly cold. The wind stopped, but it began to snow and our descent became increasingly risky. It took a tremendous effort to reach the chimney. Here we were forced to rappel. Annibale and Jack went down first and we followed taking great care to ensure the safe retrieval of our ropes. These manouevres were not easy as we all had frozen hands and feet except for Gigi, whose boots were made from reindeer leather. At six in the morning on July 20 we all finally reached Camp 3. Exhausted, we fell into the two tents and made something hot to eat.

Worried about Jack, I took care of him, massaging his feet with Foille cream. We all did our best to cheer him up. I tried to hide my fears so as not to upset the boys, but in Gigi's eyes I seemed to see the same anxious questions that nagged inside me. With Jack in this condition how were we to reach Base Camp? And what if he went on getting worse? Outside it snowed incessantly. The night was long and the tents overcrowded. At first I could not sleep because I was afraid that Jack might need something: he was moaning, his speech confused, his feet swollen and blue. On this expedition, I was acting as doctor and that, because of my companion's worrying condition, increased the strain on my nerves. But later, physical exhaustion finally overcame me and I fell asleep. My feet were very cold but I did not move for fear of disturbing my friends, and as a result, suffered slight frostbite under both my big toes.

It was not until around 11 a.m. on the morning of July 21, that we decided to go on down. Jack's feet would not go into his boots. All our boots were stiff and frozen but, with a little effort, the rest of us managed to put ours on; for Jack it was impossible. Gigi generously offered him his reindeer boots, which left him with only four pairs of socks and a pair of inner boots: it also meant he could not use crampons, so that getting down to Camp 2 became a torture for him too. On the ice slopes we had to hold his full weight because he had broken his inner boots and only had his socks left. We were about half way down the glacier when he fell towards the valley: Romano's belay could not hold him; somehow I managed to grab both their ropes and stop them. Luigino, meanwhile, was striving to find a way over the bergschrund in practically nil visibility because of the sleet and thick mist. Finally, after groping around in the snow, he found the anchors and sling that we had left. Even Romano, tired out by constantly helping Gigi, took a fall, a great flight ending below the bergschrund on a flat place which was fortunately covered with soft snow: we all ended up laughing!

We reached Camp 2: Romano, Luigino and Gigi wanted to stop, but I insisted on going on to Base Camp with Jack and Annibale since Jack's condition was really frightening. I was in fact afraid that if we waited any longer he would not be able to put his feet on the ground, and we still had to cross the steep ridge, upon which it would be impossible to carry a man. The trek was exhausting: groping in ever-thickening mist and near-darkness we reached Camp 1, where we could at last stop and sleep. Annibale's stamina seemed inexhaustible and Jack, despite his condition, was a real prodigy of moral and physical strength. We had very little food or fuel, so we resigned ourselves to melting snow with sugar and Ovaltine. With the drop in altitude, Jack improved. I massaged his feet with Gelovit, which hurt him terribly. We all spent a horrible night. Only at dawn did we manage to rest a little, while it went on snowing outside.

In the morning, around 11 a.m., we decided to go down. The fixed ropes were all covered in snow and encrusted with ice; small avalanches fell in a continual succession, but fortunately they were of very soft snow, and gave us little trouble. On the rock slabs I lost a crampon and could not catch it. Towards the end of the first couloir I was hit by a big avalanche which completely buried me but although it had come from high up, it only stunned me a little: I was still holding the fixed rope, and everything ended all right because the snow was extremely light. Unfortunately, however, I had lost the other crampon too, so the descent became even more tiring. At the end of the big couloir, the snow was so soft and deep that we sank all the way into it and had to swim our way out. It was a great relief to arrive at Base Camp!

It was another horrible night for all three of us: Jack constantly moaned because of the unbearable pain and that made us suffer too. After 75 hours of continuous snow, we finally saw the sun on the morning of July 23. Avalanches started to pour down the mountain: I thought of my friends still up there. In the evening, we were all finally united at Base Camp. After days of tension, we finally entered a state of grace, really a total relaxation of our nerves, which allowed us to savour to the full the joy of our success. From a piece of canvas with four handles on the corners we improvised a sled to carry our brave and unlucky Jack to the landing strip where Sheldon, having seen us, was waiting. He was overjoyed to discover that all six of us had climbed the route and returned safely. We immediately loaded Jack on to the plane and asked the pilot to mail the telegrams announcing our victory!

Sheldon came back next day to pick up Romano and Luigino, while Gigi, Annibale, and I stopped for another day to salvage as much gear as possible. We were all reunited in Anchorage a few days later. At the hospital Luigino, Romano and I were treated for slight frostbite, and I also had a thorough medical check. However, for Jack the period of medical care was to be long and painful. Nevertheless he recovered fully, which was most important as he was able to continue his work as a guide and ski instructor in the mountains. While I remember and write these memoirs, now that he is no longer among us*, I can see his fine, calm face again, and feel the warmth of his friendship and his generous enthusiasm for mountaineering.

Gigi, Luigino, Annibale, and Romano returned to Italy

*Jack Canali died recently in a skiing accident at Sestrieres.

before me. Whilst waiting to accompany Jack home, I went to Kotzbue to visit the incomparable Padre Spolettini. I thus had the chance to see and admire the lifestyle of the Eskimos: simple, but very impressive. Back in New York I met my dear old friend Ernani Faé. We eventually got home to Lecco on September 1.

I shall always remember the hospitality of so many friends in that distant land, of the moments of beauty and suffering during the climb, of the magnificent episodes of brotherhood and human solidarity in the realization of a marvellous dream: the conquest of the South Face of McKinley.

It was a superb victory for Lecco, and a marvellous success to mark the 15th anniversary of the formation of the 'Spiders'. It was also one of my greatest satisfactions in my long life as an alpinist, brought about by my five young companions through their dedication, their spirit of sacrifice, their discipline, and their unquestioned technical ability. I would be quite prepared to join any one of them on a major mountaineering expedition.

The expedition received far wider acclaim than just in our native city. Among other congratulations I received the following telegrams, one from the President of the United States, the other from the Italian President:

> I send my warmest congratulations to you and to the other members of the Italian team, who have achieved such a splendid mountaineering feat on Mt. McKinley. This outstanding accomplishment under the most hazardous of conditions is a fine testimonial to your superb skill and fortitude. Our nation is proud to have witnessed within its own borders this conquest which has served to strengthen the ties between the United States and Italy and to earn the admiration of all the world.
>
> JOHN F. KENNEDY

> To you and to your courageous companions comes admiring applause and deep congratulations from all Italians, and myself personally, for this successful and arduous mountaineering feat.
>
> GIOVANNI GRONCHI

CHAPTER EIGHTEEN

Climbs on Elbrus and Ushba

In 1966 through a friendly exchange between the CAI and the Russian Alpine Federation, I had the opportunity to see the Caucasus. On August 10, at 12.30, Annibale Zucchi, Paolo Consiglio, Emilio Frisia, and I took off from Milan airport. Franco Alleto joined us a few days later.

By evening we were in Moscow, where we were met by various luminaries of the Russian mountaineering world, and joined by an interpreter. The following day a four hour flight took us to Mineralnye Vody in Georgia. From here a coach took us on towards the mountains as far as Adyl-Su where, at an altitude of 1,800 metres, there was a special camp where we could stay on rest days and between expeditions.

We encountered quite a number of these camps in the Caucasus. They are used extensively by the mountaineers during their vacations, and form an important part of the Russian mountaineering system. According to individual capacity, participants are subdivided into one of five levels: routes are classified in the same manner, so that a person admitted at a particular level can't do climbs more difficult than the level to which he or she belongs.

On the coach, we visited different areas, hotels, and mineral springs along the Baksan valley, where little by little we saw the peaks and glaciers. A long ride on a funicular brought us to the slopes of Mt. Tcheget Tan Tchana (4,109 metres), where there is a rest-house. The view was spectacular: to the left was Mt. Dongusorum, with its imposing 1,500-metre wall of rock and ice, highly dangerous because of avalanches (in fact, so far, it has only been climbed once); then to the right of Mt. Tcheget towered the majestic Elbrus, which is almost always cloud-capped, but I was lucky enough to see the summit for just enough time to take a photo.

We had barely got back to our camp that night when Alletto, Toni Hiebeler, and his wife arrived. Franco, who arrived in Moscow the day after we did, had not been able to find us, and had joined the Hiebelers who had arrived in the Russian capital in their own car.

We left on our first trip into the mountains early in the morning, two days later. A truck carried us up the rough construction road towards Elbrus. We started the hut walk at 3,200 metres and just over two hours later we were at the Hut of the Eleven, at a height of 4,163 metres. It was huge, shaped like a rectangular igloo, and completely covered on the outside by sheet metal. Inside was a ground floor and two floors of sleeping quarters: it could accommodate up to 200 people. In the three days of our stay, it was always full because the groups rotated constantly. A generator supplied lighting: there was no restaurant, but the kitchen, well supplied with all sorts of pans and a wood burning stove, could be used at a reasonable cost by anyone who wanted to cook. A custodian took care of the maintenance and upkeep. My friends trickled in one at a time. While our escort made something to eat, I enjoyed the tremendous and unforgettable vista of the entire mountain chain of the Caucasus with its principal peaks: Koshtan-tau, Dykh-tau, Shkhelda, Ushba — a difficult mountain, outstandingly elegant with its towers and impressive north and west faces — Pik Shchurovsky, Dongus-oran, Filtz Zalgmil, Zamok and a jumble of others stretching to the horizon. Thus inspired we decided to go up Elbrus, time permitting, next morning.

At 1 a.m. as is customary when attempting this mountain, we left with our escort, Anatoli, and a large group of climbers from another camp. Anatoli set the pace and climbed very slowly compared with my usual speed, but I didn't know the way and it was dark so I had to stay with him. It was not at all cold; I could hear running water under the slabs of ice, but the snow was well packed and it was not a tiring walk. Around 4 a.m. we reached an altitude of 5,000 metres and at this point I moved to the head of the group to try and speed up the pace. Only Annibale kept up. After a couple of hours we reached a col where we found a permanent bivouac hut; unfortunately, it was full of snow because the door had been left open.

The wind had increased and a dense mist prevented us from finding the right way so we had to wait for the rest of the group. Annibale complained of a headache, but I felt fine. When Frisia and Anatoli reached us they were suffering from the altitude, and the escort advised us to go back because of poor visibility. However, I decided to go ahead alone. Annibale, who had recovered, joined me and at the last minute Anatoli and Frisia came too, Frisia making his task easier by leaving the pack and the movie camera at the bivouac hut. After about half an hour, the sky cleared and Annibale decided to put on his goggles to avoid snow blindness, which he had already had on Mt. McKinley. He then realized that he had left them in the pack at the bivouac, where I had left mine too. I decided to go and fetch them so that I could also bring the light meter. I went down to the bivouac hut, and back up again so quickly that by the time we reached the top, I felt unwell. Frisia also was tottering and constantly complaining about dizziness.

I took some pictures, shot a little film, and got ready to descend with the others. Anatoli roped up with Frisia while Annibale and I walked unroped along the steep slope, for the snow was beautifully firm. At the col we rested a while and were joined by four Russians who had climbed the East Peak of Elbrus. We had done the West Peak, the main one. Alletto was waiting for us at the rocks; he had climbed up there with some Russians, while Consiglio waited at the hut. The following morning we all descended to the valley.

On the 17th, after the usual meetings of our leaders, they agreed to our project to climb Ushba (4,650 metres), one of the most beautiful peaks of the Caucasus, comparable to the Matterhorn but harder, even its easiest route presenting notable difficulties. The climb involved a two-day approach march, so we had to take a tent, food and essential equipment. Our organizers tried to procure a helicopter to give us an advantage on the long walk in. During the three days that we waited, I wrote postcards and visited the various camps in the area. I noticed that the feminine element was more evident here, and that the young Russians, at least those I encountered, were very athletic and in excellent shape. Educational standards, among the young as well as older people, were high too, but their clothes left a lot to be desired.

Toni Hiebeler wanted to try a very difficult route on Ushba, but could not find anyone to follow him. Furthermore, his visitor's pass expired on the 22nd so, with great regret, he had to leave. We on the other hand prepared everything necessary, because they told us that next day a helicopter would take us to near the attack point for the face of Ushba but bad weather delayed our departure.

On the morning of August 21, in two 25 minute trips, the helicopter dropped us near a shepherds' hut at an altitude of 2,500 metres. Two old stalls were inhabited by about 15 shepherds, most of them women, who looked after a herd of 220 cattle and countless pigs. Some of these had long shaggy coats like wild boar, while others, much smaller and darker in colour, reminded me of badgers.

We all left around 8 a.m. heavily laden, and took about three hours to reach the moraine of the Ushba Glacier. Around 2 p.m. we reached a beautiful place by a mountain spring that is usually used by people who camp in the area. Ushba appeared nearby and huge and we took advantage of the marvellous day to shoot film and take pictures.

The following morning we attacked, initially by a steep snow slope that we could climb without crampons. But we had to move fast because of the danger of rockfalls from the towers of Shkhelda. On a rightward traverse, Anatoli inexplicably slipped and fell about 30 metres, by some miracle coming to rest against rocks on the edge of a 100-metre overhanging wall. We were all a little shaken by the incident. After four hours, thankfully without any more 'adventures', we arrived at the col between Shkhelda and Ushba, set up the tents, and ate. The weather turned bad and grew steadily worse until it soon became a fierce storm, followed by violent hail and snow. After about an hour, I went out to clear the tent on the uphill side, but the blizzard raged even more strongly than before. That night certainly wasn't one of the best: there were two inches of water in the tents, and everything outside was smothered in snow and hail.

The morning sky was clear, but the face of Ushba was

completely white. I took several photos and discussed what to do with my companions. The weather seemed to have stabilized and around 1 p.m. we left for the shoulder, which we reached in about two hours. While Annibale and I climbed up to fix the ropes on the first section of the wall, the others cleared a place for the tents, this time on the snow.

I traversed the face all the way to the end of the semicircular terminal bergschrund, then we climbed vertically for about 60 metres on mixed rock and ice, on rather untrustworthy ground. I then decided it would be easier to move to the left onto a steep ice-slope which we climbed for a short distance before descending to our friends, who had made something to eat.

The difficulties we had met, and above all those that I could foresee, seemed to me excessive for a team of five. Moreover it did not seem advisable to venture out in that weather, for though the next morning was clear and cold, great dark clouds appeared in the west: even the altimeter showed the change in atmospheric conditions. We contacted our guides by radio and they too advised us to come down as quickly as possible, as the weather was definitely getting worse. We returned to the meadow, where we tried in vain to get in touch by radio to see if we could summon up the helicopter but with no result. The following morning we set off on the long return trek.

Personally I was happy to walk back, as we soon found ourselves descending a valley lined with flowers and blossom, startlingly beautiful, and reaching up the sides of the mountains to an altitude of 2,800 metres. We arrived back at the camp in the evening and after a welcome shower, we had a final dinner with our hosts, with toasts and speeches of congratulation.

Before returning to Italy, we stayed in Moscow for three days, and I was able to visit most of the well-known tourist sights. I admired the immensity of Red Square, the Kremlin, the beautiful palaces, the impressive university complex, the museums, and the grandiose Gum stores. On our last night in the Soviet Union we were again guests at a large banquet with all the most important members of the Russian Alpine

Federation, among them the famous climbers Kiril Kuzmin and Vitali Abalakov. With them I drank a toast to the warm rapport between Italian and Soviet climbers, in the hope that it would continue and strengthen still further. Thus ended a most interesting foreign trip.

CHAPTER NINETEEN

Jirishanca's West Face

In 1969, I had the chance to go to the Andes, mountains that were still unknown to me. With great enthusiasm I threw myself into preparing everything necessary for an alpine-style expedition. I consulted an Andean expert, Giuseppe Dionisi, who had already been to the Peruvian Cordillera. He confirmed what I had thought, that there were no longer any important unclimbed mountains in the area. So we had to turn to some unexplored or difficult face of an already climbed peak, in order to find a result worthy of the prestige of Lecco climbers. We decided to attempt the East Face of Nevado Yerupaya (6,632 metres/21,759ft.), the highest peak in the Cordillera Huayhuash. This is a 1,200-metre ice face of a most arresting character, towering majestically above a complex icefall.

There were eight members of the expedition, most of them with experience of other important expeditions outside Europe: Gigi Alippi, Casimiro Ferrari, Giuseppe Lafranconi, Mimmo Lanzetta, Annibale Zucchi, with Sandro Liati as doctor, and myself. We left from Milan on June 6. After a short stop in Paris to change planes, we boarded a huge four-engined jet, and a fast night flight over the Atlantic brought us to Rio de Janiero at dawn and thence to Lima.

In Lima we met Cesar Morales Arnao, Professor of Andean studies, to whom I had written announcing our project. He told me that an Austrian expedition which had been unable to get a permit for the Himalayas had reached Peru unexpectedly, and was heading for the East Face of Nevado Yerupaya, exactly the same objective we had chosen. Moreover, we could not even opt for the North East Face because I had read in a French magazine that it had already been climbed by Americans the year before. It was a bad moment but after this initial upset we did some rapid research to find another equally prestigious objective. After consulting Professor Morales we decided on the West Face of Jirishanca (6,126 metres), one of the most beautiful mountains of the Cordillera Huayhuash, dubbed the 'Matterhorn of the Andes'. It is a very slender pyramid whose impressiveness and majesty are striking from any angle.

The name of my late lamented friend, the great climber Toni Egger*, is bound up with the history of this mountain. He reached the summit in 1957 by the East Face, but nobody had ever attempted our objective, the West Face, and it had developed a reputation of being inaccessible and unclimbable. To approach the base of this face, which is one single astonishing sweep of shining ice, we had to cross an unexplored glacier. Even the Klier expedition of 1954 considered it impossible.

We left on the evening of the 12th by truck and car, Professor Morales accompanying us, and the following morning, we reached the 4,200-metre Conocia Pass where an immense plain begins, scattered with lakes and marshes and teeming with duck and geese. After crossing the plain we could see the majestic Yerupaya, with Nevado Jirishanca on its left. We travelled another 30 kilometres, steadily downhill, and came to Chiquian, at an altitude of 3,553 metres. Contrary to what I expected, it is a large city of about 18,000 inhabitants, the last centre before the Cordillera.

In Chiquian we were joined by Aldoves, head of the caravan, who knew the area well, and four porters whom Morales had found for us. They had brought 40 donkeys to carry equipment and horses for us to ride. The plan was to reach Base Camp with two night halts, but each morning we lost a good deal of time finding the donkeys, which always strayed during the night, and we were unable to get an early start. As a result of these delays, we didn't reach our Base Camp site until the evening of the fourth day.

It was an idyllic spot, with two lakes, and as soon as we arrived Lanzetta took his fishing rod and caught a number of tasty trout for our dinner. My eyes wandered up the immense vista of peaks: to the left Rondoy, massive and imposing, Jirishanca's double peak, the summit of El Toro, where the

* Toni Egger died on Cerro Torre in 1959.

rocks not covered by ice had a pale rosy colour that reminded me of the Dolomites, and finally, Yerupaya's dominating, powerful mass. Each of these mountains had its own individual features, standing out crisp and sharp in the bracing air, clear and rarefied at 4,000 metres in the Andes.

Twelve days had passed since we left Italy: there was no time to lose, and I decided to leave next morning to approach our mountain with Alippi and the four porters. We walked for four hours on extremely steep and exhausting terrain until we found a suitable spot to set up an intermediate camp to serve as a deposit and supply base. After pitching a tent, we left all the equipment and provisions we had with us and returned to Base Camp, where I settled the bills with Aldoves for the transportation, and paid off the *arrieros* and their horses and donkeys. The four porters stayed, together with Arzales, the leader of the *arrieros*, who had the duty of keeping us in touch with Chiquian.

During the following days, we took turns going to the intermediate camp with food and equipment. On the 19th, it was the turn of Casimiro Ferrari, Natale Airoldi, Giuseppe Lafranconi and Annibale Zucchi who took up more equipment and another tent: the first two stayed up there while Giuseppe and Annibale came down.

The following morning, I left with Gigi Alippi and the four porters: we stopped at the intermediate camp with Morales. When the porters had gone back down Casimiro and Natale came back from their reconnaissance towards the El Toro Pass. They hadn't found a way through to the Pass and, running out of time, they left everything they had taken with them at a dump on the glacier. Next day we moved up to renew an attempt to gain the pass and set up our high camp. Morales told me that in 1957 an aeroplane, with 27 passengers on board, had crashed into the side of the col between Jirishanca and the peak of El Toro, but that after four days of vain attempts the emergency aid team had to give up searching because they could not find a way to reach the place where the plane had crashed. Gigi and Casimiro therefore decided to explore the *rognon*, which divides the El Toro glacier on the left, from the Jirishanca glacier, to see if it was shorter that way.

Later on Morales and I went up towards the Pass, following their tracks, but when we reached the point where they turned left under the icefall, hoping to find a way through, I decided to go all the way to the base of Yerupaya Chico because I had a feeling there was a better way there. But, when we were level with the place where Casimiro and Natale had left the gear, I realized it would be impossible to recover it from where we were: between us was a vast, steep slope of ice slashed by an enormous number of crevasses running in every direction, and impossible to find a way through. Even though I had been in the Karakoram and Alaska, I was impressed. I seemed to be moving through a fantastic frozen kingdom full of snares and traps. In the middle of a very long crevasse I noticed a slender snow bridge. I studied it carefully; it seemed worth the risk. I made Morales go down a few metres to belay me. Once on the bridge I could see that it supported me splendidly. My companion was not very convinced but, seeing I was well anchored, risked it himself and came over. After this, we all crossed it many times while supplying our attack camp.

The slope grew steadily steeper, and as I went higher the snow grew softer which, at an altitude of 5,000 metres, with little acclimatization, is painful. Avoiding crevasses wider than I have ever seen or imagined in all my life as a climber, we took turns breaking a trail when the snow was so deep that it touched our knees. Finally we reached the El Toro Pass and from here, I could see the south-west flank of our beautiful peak, soaring impressive and superb in its elegance.

At noon, I tried to establish radio contact as arranged, but I could not get through. Morales and I then went down towards Jirishanca, and reached a vast plateau. At this point we were no more than 200 metres from the base of the face as the crow flies. I went down along a crevasse on our right, where I thought it might be possible to get across. When we found the way, we left everything we had with us and went back, rather tired, to the intermediate camp, where Annibale and Giuseppe had just arrived. Casimiro and Dr. Liati were on their way down.

The following day, Annibale and Giuseppe left to recover the equipment, while Casimiro, Natale, Gigi and the two porters from Chiquian who had just arrived from Base Camp, set out for the high camp. I made Morales go down to Base Camp to rest, for he was feeling the effects of his exertions and his eyes were swollen because he did not like wearing goggles. I stayed at the intermediate camp to organize everything and to write. A few hours later Gigi returned with the two porters and reported that he had pitched the tent, and enthused about the face, which he thought was really impressive.

For several days our work consisted of long arduous marches from Base Camp and the intermediate camp to take supplies to the high camp. On the morning of the 23rd, after collecting everything we needed to take to the high camp, I left with Natale for the high camp. On arrival I found Annibale and Giuseppe, and from their faces I could see that they didn't feel well: reaching that high altitude too fast provoked upsets, nausea and headaches in all of us. I thought it best that we descend to recover. That evening, while the others stayed at the intermediate camp, Annibale and I continued down to Base Camp to take stock of what we had, and to send Arzales to Chiquian with a list of what to buy. He brought us back a lamb, to enliven our cuisine with fresh meat. Meanwhile the others worked on the mountain, supplying the high camp and getting started on the route itself.

On June 27 I was back at the high camp. Casimiro and Gigi were on the face. I could see them moving from 300 metres away. At around 5 p.m. they came back to camp, saying it was exhausting, and the ice was as hard as rock. They also told me that the wall above the ridge looked extremely difficult with a slope averaging 65-70 degrees, but with sections that were vertical, and the whole thing overhung by huge, terrifying encrustations of ice. We had chosen the most challenging problem of the Cordillera Huayhuash.

On June 28, four of us moved up to continue the assault, Annibale and Giuseppe fixing ropes past the point reached by Casimiro and Gigi the previous day, and Natale and I carrying the gear as well as photographing and filming. But when we were a rope's length below the previous high point, Natale and I were forced to go back because of the continuous shower of ice splinters raining down on us from the two ahead cutting steps. Also, I had finished the film and at the time the help that we could give was minor. At 6.30, when it was pitch dark, Annibale and Giuseppe returned. They had reached a point about 50 metres from the ridge, having circumvented a large serac that dominated the face and our camp as well. They reported that it didn't appear dangerous at the moment, but that was to prove untrue!

In the early hours of dawn on the 29th, Gigi Alippi and Casimiro Ferrari started out, in spite of the weather, which promised nothing good. In fact, a few hours later, the sky was completely covered and Jirishanca was hidden behind a curtain of clouds.

Around 9.30 a.m. they came back, not so much because of the weather, which was turning bad, but because of the way Gigi was feeling.

It was lucky that they did because the weather was obviously worsening, and snow set in for the day. I tried to reassure them but, in my heart of hearts I was afraid the devil was putting his fingers on us. Even the porters, who arrived after 10 a.m., kept saying '*malo tiempo*', but they said it would only last a day. I hoped they were right because life in these high camps in these conditions is boring beyond belief: you are forced to stay imprisoned in the limited space of a tent with only the alternatives of sleeping or writing. Unfortunately, for four days we were besieged by diabolical weather.

Before going to bed on July 2, I went out to look at the sky around 11 p.m. and saw that at last it had cleared, so the following day we were able to leave for the high camp to renew the attack. When we reached the high camp it was empty. I assumed that Casimiro and Sandro were on the face trying to clean out the half-covered tracks. I did not worry because I thought the two would continue for a while and then return because the weather was turning bad again. Sure enough, around 5.30 p.m. it suddenly changed and started to snow again. Frozen pellets of snow fell for more than two hours. I was worried, afraid that the pair might not have reached the tent left by Annibale and Giuseppe. Exposed to such conditions it is difficult to survive. I tried not to worry, but I could not hide my anxieties. The bad weather made us all miserable.

It was a long night, nerve-racked, insomniac. In the early hours of the morning, the sky cleared again, crisp and marvellous, but it was intensely cold. At dawn we saw, at the start of the ridge, the tent where Casimiro and Sandro had sheltered — and we breathed a sigh of relief! Since the weather had settled, I decided to let Annibale and Giuseppe move up. They climbed slowly because of their heavy loads and fresh snow. I followed their every movement, but in the little tent on the ridge there was no movement until noon: we had only heard them call in the morning. However, in the afternoon, I clearly saw Casimiro and Sandro moving, starting to climb again. They went on until 5 p.m. when they were within two pitches of the end of the ridge. Giuseppe and Annibale first reached the tent then they too climbed up the ridge to gain some crevasses where Casimiro and Sandro had found an ice cave where they could all spend the night.

Alippi, Airoldi and I packed our sacs to leave next morning, to be ready to attack as early as possible. We got up while it was still dark, drank a little milk, and by six were already on the move. Gigi led our rope, with me following and then Natale. Heavily loaded down with provisions and materials, we climbed the overhang and carried on. Several times I stopped the action to take some shots above and below us, filming one or the other of my friends in turn: not only time consuming, but really hard on the nerves. Around 3 p.m. we were on the ridge: Casimiro and Giuseppe came to help us carry our packs, which was a great relief. We climbed all the way along the ridge to the crevasse.

We all spent the night together in a huge, improbable cave like something out of Dante, filled with stalactites of ice and graceful natural architecture. I felt as if I were under the dome of a church: the sheer beauty of the place was indescribable. Unfortunately, there were seven of us for only two Nepal tents, so, from time to time, one of us had to sleep outside.

At dawn, Casimiro and Giuseppe left first: they reclimbed the first hundred metres cut the previous day until they reached the rock, visible even from below, where they placed several protection pitons. We were all anxious in this last effort to overcome the final section which separated us from the top. After a steep ice slope covered in unstable snow, which led to a ridge, we moved to the right to reach a small couloir, also full of unstable snow. We passed a small saddle, and now faced the upper part of the mushroom that forms the top of Jirishanca, of ice that was treacherous, spongy, and wind-blown on the surface. It swallowed our ice axes and gave way under our feet, denying us impetus for further movement. The fragile summit cornice seemed to want to defend the inviolability of this 6,126 metre peak. Suddenly I could no longer see Casimiro and Giuseppe, who had gone to the other side to look for a way through. Belayed by Giuseppe, Casimiro persisted, strewing his passage with chips of wood from the ice axe handle, and managed to overcome the last section to climb to the top. It was 2.30, and immediately afterwards we all reached the summit.

The cornice, fragile, never hardening because of the sun, wind and snow which constantly lash it — that ice was our sole point of contact with the earth! I was deeply moved and happy. It was an indescribable moment, such as I have experienced so many times, yet every success in the mountains has its subtle and profound nuances. With 60 years behind me, and those good lads beside me, I looked at the world from that peak: my mind seemed drugged by infinite silence. Our exchanged embraces were almost silent, each of us in complete unity with the mountain below us.

I took some pictures after we had unpacked the flags of Lecco, the Spiders, and others, symbolizing and recording our affection and friendship. We did not have much time to rest: we had to go down as soon as possible so as not to risk staying the night out on the face where there was nowhere to bivouac. Gigi and Sandro started the descent and were already quite low when Casimiro and Giuseppe followed.

73 Typical mixed ground on the upper section of the Cassin Ridge. This photo was taken above Camp 3 during the final summit push.

74 (top left) the final summit slopes of Mt. McKinley.

75 (left) The team pose on the summit in bitterly cold conditions.

76 (above) Zucchi and Canali at Base Camp after an epic descent.

77 Don Sheldon discussing flight plans with Cassin. Zucchi is squeezed into the back of the fully laden aircraft.

78 A view from Ushba, past Shkhelda to Elbrus in the Caucasus. The climbers are (left to right) Annibale Zucchi, the Soviet guide Anatoli, Paolo Consiglio, Franco Alletto and Emilio Frisia.

79 The Italian Jirishanca team: (left to right) Natale Airoldi, Gigi Alippi, Annibale Zucchi, Mimmo Lanzetta

80 Rondoy, Jirishanca and Yerupaya Chico. The route drops to the glacier from the El Toro Pass (behind the spur on the right), a diversion forced on the climbers by the dangerously complex state of the main icefall in the foreground.

81 The West Face of Jirishanca in the Cordillera Huayhuash of the Peruvian Andes.

82 The 3000 metre South Face of Lhotse, one of the most challenging problems of the Nepal Himalaya. In 1975, before any similar Himalayan wall had been climbed, the choice of this face as an objective can now be seen as very advanced. Cassin and his team changed their plans after close study of its considerable dangers, opting for a less serious line on the face to the left. In 1981 a Yugoslav team, with experience of similar routes on Makalu and Everest, climbed a direct line up the face to the foot of the final rock wall.

84 Whillans Boxes at Camp 1 on Lhotse — Ama Dablam is the peak in the background.

83 (left) The ice ridge above Camp 1 on Lhotse.

85 Avalanche devastation at Base Camp.

86 (below) The Italian route on the South Face of Lhotse. Only three camps were actually placed, the site for Camp 4 was chosen however, and is marked here. The climbers had hoped to use Camp 4 as a jump-off point for a push along the skyline ridge to the summit.

87 A sherpa moving up fixed ropes on the steep ice walls above Camp 2.

88 The Italian Lhotse Expedition: (left to right — standing) Gigi Alippi, Sereno Barbacetto, Riccardo Cassin, Franco Gugiatti, Aldo Leviti, Ignazio Piussi, Reinhold Messner, Alessandro Gogna, Fausto Lorenzi and Mario Curnis; (kneeling) Giuseppe Alippi, Mario Conti and Gianni Arcari.

89 Buckled tent poles at Camp 3 after the avalanche that nearly killed Barbacetto and Leviti.

90 Reinhold Messner on the rock slabs above Camp 3 on Lhotse.

Annibale, Natale and I were moving slower because there were three of us and we had to retrieve the ropes. It was already dark when we reached the god-sent crevasse, helped by the light of our friends' torches. The bivouac had the intoxicating smell of success. I shared the little Nepal tent with the other two, yet it felt more comfortable than the day before; the underlying ice seemed almost soft and less cold, for my nerves were so strung out after days of anxiety and hope, of moments so intensely experienced and suffered.

In the morning we went down to the base of the face. The porters came to meet us, welcoming us with great emotion and helping us carry our heavy packs to the high camp. We decided to leave immediately for Base Camp even though it was a long way. I told the porters to load up the items we needed most and leave the rest to be recovered later. Around 5.30, we were at the intermediate camp. At first there were hints that some of us wanted to stay there, but in the end everyone opted for the comfort and space of Base Camp, which we reached when it was already dark. A huge and much desired spaghetti was washed down with white wine, and we went to bed positively euphoric with the combination of wine and exhaustion. In the following days, while we waited for Ardoves to return with the burros, the various camps were packed up, and we idled away our time fishing before leaving for Chiquian, and eventually Italy, on July 11.

That extraordinary, miraculous West Face of Jirishanca, with the extreme difficulties presented by its new route, had satiated me, thanks to the courage of my young companions. Once again Man, at the limit of his abilities, had won the fight against ice, storms, and the bitter cold.

CHAPTER TWENTY

Defeat on Lhotse

During the assembly of delegates from the Italian Alpine Club, that met in Milan on May 27, 1973, I introduced the subject of climbing outside Europe. Expressing regret that there had been no more organized national expeditions since K2, Gasherbrum IV and the Antarctic, I proposed Lhotse (8,501 metres/27,890ft.), the fourth highest mountain in the world, as the goal of the next expedition, and asked for the backing of the Assembly, the Central Committee, and the Italian Government. I said that I already had permission for access to the South Face of Lhotse in the pre-monsoon period of 1975.

At this time mountaineering expeditions outside Europe were undergoing an evolution similar to that years ago in the Alps when, after the exploratory phase had exhausted itself, attention turned to more difficult ridges, faces, and aretes. The South Face of Lhotse was the greatest remaining problem; the choice of this extremely difficult face was recognised by the CAI Assembly, and the project received its full backing. It would be the fourth national CAI expedition of a scientific and mountaineering nature.

In the spring of 1974, I was in Nepal to make the first reconnaissance to the base of the face on foot, with my friend Roberto Sorgato, of Belluno. Thus I had the chance to photograph the mountain repeatedly from an altitude of about 5,300 metres. I was also able to choose a possible site for our Base Camp at the foot of the face.

The same place had been chosen by four preceding expeditions, and answered all the necessary requirements: moreover, the various phases of the climb on that stupendous South Face, with its superb 3,000 metre vertical wall, would be visible from this point. Though it would be a hard job, difficult and perhaps impossible, I saw no traces that led me to suspect avalanche danger on the face because there were no signs of debris or avalanches at the bottom. I was aware of the Japanese attempt in 1973: they had reached an altitude of 7,000 metres on the South Face, but well over to the left of the ideal route I had chosen.

It was worth the effort of trying it, and whatever happened, Italians would have the credit of having tried first. Thoughts of Whymper and Mummery came to mind:

"It is always more glorious to fail on a peak that has not been climbed than to fail on a second attempt of a route already done."

In October of the same year I had the opportunity to make an aerial reconnaissance, and thus confirmed that the wall would be extremely hard. But if nobody attempted it, I told myself, the problem would always be unresolved. If fortune were to favour us a little with good weather, we would stand a good chance of pulling it off. Before returning to Italy, I checked the equipment left us by the CAI expedition from Bergamo; I also had the chance to acquire propane and oxygen cylinders from the French expedition, whose attempt on the complete West Ridge of Everest had had to be called off after an enormous avalanche killed Gérard Devouassoux, leader of the expedition, and five Sherpas.

I invited 15 people on the expedition, trying to choose the cream of Italian climbers. Some could not accept because of their work, but in the end the team was a very strong one comprising myself as leader, Franco Chierego (doctor), Giuseppe Alippi (nicknamed Det), Aldo Anghileri, Giovanni Arcari, Gigi Alippi, Sereno Barbacetto, Mario Conti, Mario Curnis, Alessandro Gogna, Franco Gugiatti, Aldo Leviti, Fausto Lorenzi, Reinhold Messner and Ignazio Piussi. They were a formidable team who, as well as being fine climbers to the man, had a keen sense of duty, obedience, and tenacity of purpose, to such an extent that I was sure that as far as the human element was concerned, we could only come out of it well.

We left Italy on March 10, 1975 on two military aeroplanes, Hercules C130s. One carried supplies and materials, the other all the expedition members except Alessandro Gogna who, having left with his wife a few months before by train from Yugoslavia to Iran, Pakistan and then Nepal, had already arrived in Kathmandu. My years, and experience acquired on previous expeditions particularly heightened the last moments before take-off. Again I was leading a group of young men in an attempt to solve an important mountaineering problem outside Europe. I felt calm: I knew I had prepared everything that might contribute to the success of this attempt with shrewd, meticulous care. I had that vivid enthusiasm I always have whenever I set out on a new adventure, a tough battle between me and a mountain. Are not the things that are most difficult to achieve perhaps the most significant to our existence?

After an intermediate stop at New Delhi, we reached Kathmandu on the morning of the 12th. Waiting to welcome us, besides the Gognas, were Dr. Fimiani, head of the Italian Embassy, and Colonel Ondgi, who was to organize transport for us to Lukla and for our materials to Base Camp. Next morning I went to the Foreign Ministry for our Trekking Permit: here I had the opportunity of a long talk with the Director, Dr. Khannal, a very courteous official who did all he could within the limits of his capacity to help me resolve various problems. Unfortunately, the hope of ham radio communication direct to Italy disappeared because the Ministry rules clearly forbid it. All the same, I managed to obtain permission to communicate by radio through the Anglo-Nepalese expedition on Nuptse, so we could send news to Kathmandu every two days. In practice, due to the distance between the two camps and a series of interferences on the transmission channels, I had to fall back on the traditional mailman.

Mr. Khannal approved the clearance of the materials without any difficulty; he also told me that a Himalayan Mountaineering Club had been formed and would like advice and suggestions because they intended to set up climbing schools for Sherpas and also form a group of climbers to initiate real outdoor sports, as in Europe. I assured him that I would gladly place myself at his disposal to collaborate, and study the possibility, if necessary, of sending one of our instructors. Dr. Khannal also introduced me to Naati

Chottare, the Sherpa who was to be our liaison officer. He was from Kathmandu and had been on several expeditions. He was *sirdar* to the Japanese expedition, when he reached the summit of Everest. Due to his particular mountaineering skill he had been promoted to liaison officer. Gogna, Giorgetta and I went to the office of the Foreign Minister to pay for the permission to clear customs: they asked for five copies, in English, of the equipment lists for each carton. We had a mass of Italian copies, but only three in English. We lost precious time resolving this bureaucratic obstacle because there was nowhere in Kathmandu to make photo-copies: Colonel Ondgi's backing was a great help to us, for he knew everything and everyone.

On the 15th the first part of the expedition, comprising Reinhold Messner, Mario Conti and Aldo Anghileri, left for Lukla and the following day Gigi Alippi, Sereno Barbacetto, Aldo Leviti, Ignazio Piussi and Giuseppe Alippi followed. The remaining members and myself followed a couple of days later.

When we landed at Lukla, on the famous sloping dirt runway, I gathered from our *sirdar*, Ang Tsering, that the other members of the expedition had already left for Namche Bazar. In the morning we set out on the trail with several porters, taking some supplies and equipment with us. Phakding Khola, the first place we reached, lies in an area rich with beautiful conifers. At the sight of the clear cool water of a river, I could not resist jumping in to freshen up. The places that we passed through were truly fascinating: a variety of bridges to cross, characterized by their primitive architectural beauty, wonderful valleys with rich conifers, and native villages. In the most sheltered areas, in spite of the altitude and the early season, we found enormous rhododendrons which, unlike ours at home, were already in bloom.

We reached Namche Bazar on the 20th and found our friends. Then, divided into groups, we set out for Thyangboche. I left with Sherpa Phurbu, whom I had had the year before on my reconnaissance with Sorgato. Messner joined me after overseeing the departure of the yaks carrying our baggage. We quickly covered the distance to Thyangboche and visited a monastery where five or six Lamas were living. The next stretch was to Pheriche, but our medicine had not yet arrived and several of us had colds and coughs. I consulted our doctor, our friend Chierego, who quite correctly said that leaving without medicine was a risk, a responsibility he preferred not to assume, and so Franco Gugiatti offered to return to Namche with two porters to pick up the necessary.

On Monday March 24, Franco Chierego, Aldo Anghileri and I crossed to Pangpoche to look for the grave of Paolo Consiglio, who died there in 1973. We found it further on, in the Tsuro region, an hour's walk from Dingpoche. Sadly, the sky was always overcast and the peaks covered by cloud. Towards evening, it started to snow and everything was blanketed in white. We pitched camp near a farm on a plateau at an altitude of 4,300 metres.

Next morning we woke to find ten centimetres of fresh snow. The *sirdar* of our trekking party was worried that his porters, men and women, had no suitable equipment and proposed to take everyone down; we went ahead anyway, taking the cooks and attendants with us. It snowed all day but the following morning, around eleven, the clouds began to thin out and the peaks appeared. Curnis and I went up the mountain on the right, in front of Ama Dablam; before us were the magnificent peaks I had already seen, though from a different angle. Curnis and I climbed up the steep slope to an altitude of 4,800 metres and I took some shots of the majestic Thamserku (6,608 metres), Taboche (6,542 metres), Kangtega (6,779 metres), which is in front of Ama Dablam (6,856 metres), and of Lobuche (6,119 metres), still on the left of the Khumbu Valley.

On Thursday March 27, despite the beautiful weather, we had to stop and wait for our baggage and equipment before we could finally leave for Dingboche. Lhotse was totally black and, seeing it from the west, the boys were highly impressed by the wall's imposing nature. During my April reconnaissance, I had never seen it black like that: all the time I had been there with Sorgato, it snowed almost every day; then in October, during my aerial reconnaissance, it had seemed possible, even though, as I had always maintained, it also seemed very difficult.

The place chosen for Base Camp was magnificent, on the tongue of the moraine. Everybody arrived in dribs and drabs: Chierego, feeling terrible, arrived last. I made him get into the tent immediately, and made hot tea for him. He didn't want to eat. We settled in as best we could, ate and then withdrew to our tents. But Chierego was not at all well. I made him tell me the drugs that might help him, and Mariolino and I set off to find the boxes they were in. That night he was racked by continual nausea and vomiting. I consulted the others and we decided that if he didn't get better, we would take him lower down. Meanwhile, I gave him some oxygen but it did no good. Next day, we improvised a stretcher because ours were still on the way up and, on difficult terrain covered by fresh snow, we managed to transport our unlucky medic to Dingpoche, where he was treated by the Anglo-Nepalese doctor, then to the Kathmandu hospital. From there he went back to Italy.

Unfortunately, on this first short stop at Base Camp, the South Face started to discharge not just snow but rock and ice. Because of one particularly massive fall the face went completely black. Everything that fell disappeared into enormous crevasses at the base of the wall, so that there was no sign of how much did come down. That was the harsh reality that faced us under this great wall! Contrary to my suppositions, it was dangerously treacherous, and attempting it in those conditions would be suicidal. We therefore held a conference to decide on another way to climb up the enormous icy spur which ran diagonally up the left side of the wall. The only vulnerable point was the route already attempted by the Japanese, who reached an altitude of 7,000 metres.

The boys prepared the necessary gear for the first reconnaissance, and on the morning of April 1, Messner, Gogna and Anghileri left, while Gugiatti and I went up the spur on the front to take a last look at the face to see if there was any remote possibility of climbing up the central spur. However, the face was completely white because of the recent snowfall.

Studying it so closely with binoculars, I immediately noticed the great difficulty there would be in pitching a camp, especially on the lower levels. The previous night's snow precipitated a continuous torrent of avalanches which seldom reached the bottom, disappearing into thin air on their way down: but even the light ones swept away anything they came across.*

Gugiatti and I went on to an altitude of 5,600 metres and moved rightwards trying to spot our friends who were climbing: we heard them talking and banging in pitons but we couldn't see them. We climbed down, and at 12.30 I made radio contact with them: they told me they had reached 5,800 metres, that everything was going well, and that they had found traces of the Japanese expedition-ropes embedded in the ice, making them useless. In the 2 p.m. transmission, they said they had reached 5,950 metres and had seen, a little higher up, a place under a spur of rock for Camp 1. When we all met together for dinner, we had to decide who would go back up with the porters to establish Camp 1: Sandro Gogna again, with Fausto Lorenzi; Franco Gugiatti with Giuseppe Alippi; while Aldo Leviti was to go as far as the second tower with three Sherpas, so as to return before the others, since he would stay at Camp 1 with Reinhold Messner next day.

On April 2, Messner and Lorenzi reached the place where Camp 1 was to be established, while the others fixed ropes and enlarged the ice steps to help the Sherpas, who were carrying heavy loads. They went on to fix ropes until late afternoon, and then came down. That evening a heavy fall of snow covered everything in white again, but I was not worried because the boys were all in camp; what did worry me was the rest of the gear which we were still waiting for. We ate dinner separated in various tents because they had not yet brought up the big one which would serve as the mess tent.

The following morning, Messner and Leviti left very early, and were followed later by four Sherpas. They established Camp 1 at an altitude of 6,000 metres, and settled in while the porters returned. I went down to Chukhung with Gugiatti to

* In May 1981, a very strong Yugoslav expedition, led by Ales Kunaver, succeeded in climbing the South Face to a point some 500ft. below the summit. Full expedition siege tactics were used, and the climb proved to be very difficult. Source: *Mountain 80*.

find out the transport situation, and during the trip I managed to keep radio contact with Base Camp and my friends on the face. At Pheriche, I met the Englishmen on the Nuptse expedition: they were very kind to us, especially since we now had no doctor, and promised to help us as far as they could whenever we needed them, for their Base Camp was quite near ours. Very early the following morning, the porters arrived with baggage yaks from other valleys and passes and so, around 10 a.m. we all left with our equipment.

Meanwhile Messner and Leviti had slept at Camp 1 and fixed ropes up another 300 metres. Lorenzi and Curnis took them another 400 metres of rope and returned to Camp 1 where they stayed with two Sherpas, while Messner and Leviti returned to Base Camp.

On April 5 the weather stayed fine, seeming to be on our side for once. Gogna and Barbacetto fixed ropes all the way up to the bottom of the serac, where they worked hard to find a way out. I climbed up to Base Camp, where all the loads arrived in dribs and drabs: only one package and the large mess tent were missing. In the afternoon we started to organize the baggage, trying to find the most essential equipment and supplies. It was a little difficult to find the things we were looking for among 700 mixed packages, although there was a list of contents on each one. It was almost dark when we finished.

The following morning, Curnis and Anghileri set off with the two Alippis (who were to come down that night while the other two switched with Gogna and Barbacetto), but they could not reach the spot we had picked out for Camp 2. At Base Camp meanwhile, we tried to reorganize the loads that had just arrived, including our large mess tent, which we immediately pitched. We set up a table in the centre and put our supplies in there. We were also anxiously awaiting the mail, which was due at any moment. Those who received something grinned in satisfaction, while the others were quite disappointed. On top of that, the lucky ones made fun of those who had nothing, like a children's game!

One of the many altercations with the Sherpas arose: one of them had no inflatable mattress or whatever. Often, these disagreements grew out of a misunderstanding. The language difference was too great: even if some of them understood a little English, they often misinterpreted the few words they knew. Fortunately, we could almost always come to an agreement, often by giving in or conceding what they wanted.

In the following days quick sorties were made by various ropes, alternating to equip and establish Camp 2. Everyone contributed to the final result enthusiastically, capably and seriously, trying in every way to smooth out any difficulties. I was very pleased with all my boys, not only with their climbing, but also with them as people, a very important factor in an expedition as committing as ours. Only Anghileri did not want to stay any longer, and asked to return to Italy; this disappointed me deeply. We had already been left without a doctor who had left against his will because of his health; now this departure came up unexpectedly, and greatly compromised the progress of the expedition. Who can say whether with Anghileri, or some other effective climber whose coveted place he had usurped, we might not have had a more satisfactory outcome. His was a gesture that caused me great grief, and somewhat discredited us as representatives of Italian alpinism.

On the night of the 8th it snowed, and in the morning we found more than 20 centimetres of snow; it had drifted in the wind so we couldn't calculate exactly how much had fallen. Moreover, the weather did not look like changing so in our radio contact with Camp 1, I advised everybody to come down to Base Camp. We passed a dreamy and monotonous day, writing and going from one tent to another, but my young companions got on really well together, always ready to fool around during every pause in the work, which made for a pleasantly relaxed atmosphere.

The following morning, the weather turned good again, though it was very cold and there was a strong wind. We decided to go up. Gugiatti and Det went to Camp 1 with six Sherpas, while Leviti followed them that afternoon. On April 11, Reinhold and Aldo reached Camp 2, at an altitude of 6,600 metres; they pitched the Whillans Box at the beginning of a hanging glacier and camped there for the night. But the

Sherpas then announced that they were not going to climb the next day because their Lama's book said it would be bad, so they came down from Camp 1 to Base Camp. I talked to our *sirdar* and he promised to go personally with three Sherpas to take Messner and Leviti what they needed.

That night was bitterly cold, and very windy. From Base Camp, I radioed the two upper camps at 7.30 in the morning. Radio contact was certainly precious to us: any problem of supplies could be quickly solved, and the men on the wall felt they were being supported and were closer to us, while I could co-ordinate the various movements and give advice or suggestions when necessary. When I talked to Gugiatti at Camp 1, he confirmed that everything was ready to go up and he was waiting for the Sherpas. I contacted Messner at Camp 2, and he told me that they had been kept awake all night by a howling gale.

During the next radio contact at 12.30, Leviti calmed me down: unlike where we were, up there the wind had almost stopped and, things being the way they were, he told me they were thinking of going early that afternoon to make a reconnaissance of the route ahead. However, they were impatiently waiting for the porters with the Box, ropes and supplies. In the last radio contact at 6 p.m., I learned that the three Sherpas had arrived, the other Box had been pitched, and they had been higher than Camp 2 and seen that there were no excessive difficulties as far as the bottom of the ridge.

The two Sherpas who had been at Camp 1 had come down, leaving only the younger one up there. I complained to Ang Tsering, who assured me they would leave before the sahibs in the morning so as to reach Camp 2 at the same time. On the night of the 12th there was a tremendous wind at Camp 2. Messner told me that they had a strong impression that the wilder gusts would blow the tent away. I told him that the two Sherpas had left early and that Curnis and Lorenzi would climb up at 8 a.m. to relieve them. Reinhold answered that at the moment they could not move and they would see what the situation was like later. At the 12.30 radio contact, I learned that the wind up there was still very strong and they still could not get out of the tent. I told them that Curnis and Lorenzi were two hours away from the camp.

Messner and Leviti came down, and in fact met Lorenzi and Curnis an hour from Camp 2: they established the time for the next radio contact at 5.30 and reached Base Camp as hungry as wolves. At the agreed time, I heard that the visibility was minimal and the wind still blowing wildly. They asked for the most essential items for the camp, which would have to become an Advance Base Camp. Because of this, Piussi started working out the possibility of installing a cableway to transport the materials and supplies: it was the steepest and most difficult stretch, where the Sherpas could not make it with their loads, to such an extent that they sometimes abandoned them *en route.* Around 6 p.m., I found that the two Sherpas who should have stayed at Camp 1 and gone on to Camp 2 the following morning, had come down instead. I talked to the *sirdar* again and he assured me that he himself, with two other Sherpas, would replace them.

During the night the wind calmed down somewhat, and even the cold eased off. Looking up, however, we could see that it was still blowing hard: it was a torment of snow. In fact this was confirmed by Lorenzi in the 7.30 radio contact with Camp 2:

"There's an insane storm up here and it's still snowing. Last night was really exceptional; even the tent was blown apart. We're going to come down and wait for the weather to change."

I advised them to fix the tents as best they could and come down as soon as possible. Curnis, Lorenzi and Leviti, who had taken part in the Monzino Expedition to Everest in 1973, said that throughout their stay in Base Camp and the higher camps, they had never seen such weather. When the sun had been out, they had stayed outside half-naked: for that matter for the first eight to ten days, even we had had good days. But now, the weather was doing its worst.

On the morning of the 15th, the sky was still overcast: during the night, the wind had blown hard higher up, while at Base Camp it snowed. A group of Sherpas left for Camp 1; Gogna and Barbacetto were to follow later, but about an hour later the weather got worse and before noon it was already snowing, so the pair had to postpone their projected departure. Piussi, helped by the two Alippis and Arcari, worked on the cableway, gathering everything he needed to set it up: it had to be placed halfway between Camp 1 and Camp 2 so we tried to build up as much gear as possible at Camp 1 to equip the higher camps.

Taking advantage of a marvellous day, after finally having one calm night without wind, eight Sherpas left for Camp 1 on Thursday April 17, with rope and accessories for the cableway. Piussi, Arcari, and the two Alippis followed them to help get it working. The same morning Gogna and Barbacetto, who had reached Camp 1 the previous afternoon, went up to Camp 2 and planned to open the route to Camp 3 the following day. Conti came up with me: I was heavily loaded, carrying a movie camera, which was very heavy, two stills cameras, the canteen, and various other things. It was a shame that the mist around 11 a.m. stopped me filming those truly fantastic panoramas and horizons. Camp 1 was in a beautiful position on a ridge with a stupendous view. Towards evening, we went down after taking some pictures.

On Friday, in absolutely beautiful weather, everyone got moving very early to carry out the various tasks they had been given: one group was to mark the route and another to set up the cableway. In the afternoon, Gugiatti and Leviti left for Camp 1 and thence to Camp 2; Messner and Lorenzi were going straight to Camp 2. I spotted Barbacetto and Gogna quite high on the glacier above Camp 2, and in the 3 p.m. radio contact, Gogna told me they had reached an altitude of 7,100 metres.

That night it snowed. Talking to Camp 2, I heard from Gogna that 25 centimetres of fresh snow had fallen. They had tried to make their way to Camp 3, but they had not even managed to reach the previous day's high point. Even the Sherpas, after having reached Camp 1, didn't finish the jobs given to them: in fact three should have gone with Leviti and Gugiatti to Camp 2, but they wasted time and left their loads halfway between the two camps.

During the evening radio communication, I gathered the day's news:

"Base Camp calling One. If you hear me, answer. Out."

Piussi answered: "Loud and clear. Out."

"How did the cableway set-up go today?" I asked. "Tell me everything."

"It went fine today, we managed to get the pulley from the ridge to the starting point under Camp 1. But it went a bit wrong yesterday. We carried it up on our backs and lowered it down. Then we had a silly accident and it ended up in a crevasse and we couldn't get it back. But we managed today and we've anchored it, as I was telling you, below Camp 1, the one we're going to substitute for your camp later."

"Good, that's great news," I replied, and closed down. We went to sleep quite happy, satisfied with the results so far. It was 9 p.m. on April 19.

Around midnight, I heard a great rumbling and a crash, followed by a terrific wind. Someone was calling: I switched a torch on to see the whole tent was flattened. I shook it and could feel it heavy with snow. I went out and saw Messner, half-dressed and covered in snow dust: the rush of air and the snow from an avalanche down the Lhotse Face had demolished his tent and damaged the Sherpas' tents and mine too. Reinhold was invited into Conti's tent and I went back to mine, though the ridge pole was broken: I decided to fix it in the morning.

At around 6 a.m. I crawled out to inspect the damage in daylight. I looked around and saw Messner's tent on the ground and the rest of the damage. I scrutinized the face to see where the avalanche had come from, but I could not pinpoint it exactly because it had snowed lightly. I went back to my tent and my rest. I don't know how much time had passed when, half asleep, I heard another great rumble, a tremendous roar and a crash, and then a fierce wind hit everything. I felt a huge weight run quickly over me: instinctively, I threw my arms over my head immediately to protect myself and tried to get up, but I was sucked down again straight away.

I have no idea how long that inferno lasted! When everything seemed to have calmed down, I laboriously managed to wriggle out of my tent. It was a terrifying sight: I could see nothing of our precious village of tents. Everything had vanished, as if a monstrous bulldozer had levelled it all, leaving only a thick blanket of snow. The first things I saw were Messner and Conti, completely white from head to foot. With them, I went to the Sherpa tents where we heard moans. With ice axes and knives, we freed the imprisoned Sherpas: one was breathing heavily; some were hurt, but fortunately not seriously. We managed to dry them off a little with towels, for they were soaking and covered with snow, and tried to recover some sleeping bags as quickly as possible to cover them up a bit, since it was bitterly cold.

The boxes of our equipment and supplies, and the 30-kilo gas cylinders were scattered in a radius of more than a kilometre round where the camp had been.

I tried to contact my friends at Camps 1 and 2, but not until 7.30, the time of the usual transmission, could I make myself heard. When I finally got through, I understood their total astonishment. They were completely unaware of anything, even the men at Camp 1, who could normally see Base Camp with the naked eye. Since it had snowed lightly, it seemed to the camps above that that was why everything was white: it looked perfectly normal. I asked them all to come down immediately to help us.

While the sun came out and the temperature grew milder, everyone tried to find his own things: we spent three days searching for our clothes and personal effects which were strewn all over the glacier. Fortunately for us, there were only five climbers at Base Camp with about 15 Sherpas, cooks and attendants; otherwise the consequences would surely have been much more serious.

Our friends from Camp 1 reached us around 9.30. We were immediately worried about whether or not the Sherpas intended to continue on the expedition. They seemed to want to go on, so we met to decide whether to continue ourselves or stop and return to Italy. However, we were missing the four from Camp 2 who had not yet arrived. A decision had to be made. If we decided to return to Italy, a temporary Base Camp would have to be established in the valley; if we continued with the expedition, we would have to put it somewhere not only immune from danger, but also functional and permanent. We took an inventory of the equipment left and when the others arrived we decided, almost unanimously, to continue. We checked all the tents: some had to be discarded, others were repairable. Towards evening, we succeeded in moving the camp and organizing the reserve tents at the new Base Camp, displaced to the left on the slopes of the buttress under the South Face.

Our wounded improved, and next afternoon the local porters who were to move the gear from the old to the new camp arrived. Conti, after his shower of snow from the avalanche, relapsed into the bronchitis that he had seemed to have overcome; Lorenzi, afflicted by fierce constipation, had difficulty breathing too, so I gave both of them permission to go down to Namche Bazar. Meanwhile, two Englishmen from the Nuptse expedition reached us with a note from their doctor: their oxygen cylinders were still in customs and they needed a couple for therapeutic reasons. I was happy to be able to repay them at least partially for all their kindness, and gave them the cylinders, equipped with an American-style automatic face mask. Unlike the French type, these supply oxygen only in proportion to the need of the person being treated. In the evening, while it was snowing, after hours of strenuous work, we celebrated Piussi's birthday. This developed into a pretty boisterous party so, at the end, with a certain amount of heavy authority, I had to calm down the festivities and send them all to bed.

The weather was marvellous on the morning of the 22nd, but it didn't fool me because it snowed almost every afternoon. After breakfast, the people whose turn it was should have gone to Camp 1 to resume the climb, but the Sherpas refused to work because the Lama had said it was a bad day. So we had to postpone everything until the next day. This sort of thing was very irritating, for I realized that we were wasting one of the precious days still left before the monsoon arrived, and already there were very few of them. Towards evening, however, all the gear had been transported to the new Base Camp, except for the oxygen cylinders and the things that could remain uncovered: we would pick those up on the way to the higher camps as we needed them. On the 23rd, we were busy organizing and dividing up the supplies and materials and preparing the loads for the Sherpas who were going to follow the climbers. In the afternoon, Messner, Curnis and Piussi set off for Camp 1: next day the first two would go to Camp 2 and on towards Camp 3, while Piussi was to stop at the top of the cableway to fix the cable.

The following morning, the two Alippis and Arcari left to help set up the cableway, with Sherpas who had supplies for the advance camps. Last thing, around 6.30, Gianni returned to Base, while Gigi and Det stayed at Camp 1 to go on to the higher camp next day. I turned on the radio and Curnis immediately answered from Camp 2, where 80 centimetres of new snow had fallen. It had taken the group eight hours to reach him and only two of the four porters had arrived. The other two had come down because they could not manage the trip. Around 7 p.m., Piussi arrived at Camp 1 and, in a voice so hoarse that I could hardly understand it, announced that if all went well, the cableway would be working next day.

The morning of the 25th was marvellous: I prayed that the weather would last and allow us to do what we wanted so much. In the first radio contact, Gigi told me he intended to go to Camp 2 with Det after putting the final touches to the cableway, but he would decide that with Messner and Curnis, who were better able to judge the snow conditions. Messner thought it very dangerous to stay in Camp 2 alone and wanted to see if it were possible to go up to Camp 3 that same day, or more sensible to wait until the snow either settled or was blown away by the wind. To tell the truth, he was quite pessimistic about continuing within the next few hours.

Having heard what Gogna and Barbacetto had said, I also advised him to take great care. "You must watch out, especially on that slope — it's very steep, and it might avalanche on top of the tents," I radioed and, still in contact with Reinhold, passed the earpiece to Barbacetto so that the two of them could communicate directly. This sense of responsibility and friendly, fraternal co-operation that all of us, from the oldest to the youngest, felt for each other was a heart-warming and also extremely important side to our expedition. Even if I stand accused of being too weak and kind and therefore unsuitable as leader of a modern expedition, I want to point out that this rather paternal manner of mine in leading expeditions has, in the past, always given me great satisfaction in equally great victories. More than anything, it has paved the way to increasing and deepening our friendships when we returned home, unlike what has happened on many other expeditions whose members have ended up enemies.

The morning's good weather disappeared; at noon the sky was covered, and at 2 p.m. it started to snow. "If it continued like this," I thought, "I don't know how they'll get out." Piussi and Det arrived towards evening, tired but satisfied because, before coming down, they had sent up the first load on the cableway. This would certainly be a great advantage to us. However, we had to wait for the snow to go. In the meantime, we carried materials and supplies to Camp 2 to be ready for good weather. The 26th conformed to the usual meteorological pattern: a cloudless sky in the morning, snow in the afternoon! From Camp 2, Curnis told me Messner was not feeling well and on Gugiatti's advice I sent a Sherpa up to Camp 1 with the appropriate medicine; Gigi could then send it on up the cableway. Reinhold was better after a few hours' rest, but I recommended him to come down as soon as possible while Leviti, Gogna, and Barbacetto left from Base Camp to meet him in case he could not continue alone. Later Messner was feeling much better, and with Curnis reached the top of the cableway in a relatively short time, despite the deep snow. Conti and Lorenzi also returned fit from their five days in Namche Bazar. However, the bad weather continued, with quite heavy snow.

On the 27th, the weather improved, but there were strong winds and avalanches that poured continuously down the face. The wind was gusting very strongly at both Camps 1 and 2. Leviti, who had climbed with Gogna to the start of the cableway, said that it was snowing on top, while down where we were, it was only cloudy. During the night the wind rose, gusting strongly, and I distinctly heard the uproar caused by avalanches crashing down from the walls of Lhotse. In the morning the weather was beautiful again; however, higher up, the face was completely swathed in whirling snow. In fact, in our first contact with the higher camps, Barbacetto told me that there had been a gale all night that had blown away the layer of snow beneath the tent so that they had felt they were about to be whisked away with everything else at any moment. On the other hand, Gogna and Leviti had had a quiet night in a tent at the end of the cableway, where it was more sheltered. Around 11 a.m., the wind dropped so they immediately set to work sending gear up, even manipulating the winch without the Sherpas who usually did it.

On April 30, the wind had calmed down at Camp 1, but was still blowing hard at 2: Gogna and Leviti told me the tents were semi-buried in the snow, and that it would take all day to free them. For practical purposes the weather from April 20 to May 2 was always bad, forcing us into inactivity. We couldn't go beyond Camp 2 because it snowed every night, preventing us from going further. The morning of May 3 looked good: the weather was fine and there was no wind even high up. In the first radio contact, Camp 2 told me they were thinking of leaving for Camp 3 in a group of four with the same number of Sherpas. At Camp 1, Lorenzi had a sore throat again, so Arcari went down to replace him to keep the loads moving on the cableway.

At 8 a.m., as arranged, I turned on the radio to find myself listening to Messner.

"We couldn't get one of the Sherpas up — he said he couldn't stand up. But we'll try to go up with a tent and everything we need. But with only three Sherpas, it'll be hard to carry everything for the camp and enough gear to work with tomorrow."

"Yes, you're right," I answered, "you'll just have to do the best you can; I'd say still to go up with the three. The two Sherpas who are coming back will have to return tomorrow and bring you the rest."

"O.K. by me," said Reinhold, "two can stay at the cableway; but they must send the other Sherpas who are coming up with the radio, otherwise there won't be one at Camp 2."

"Fine," I confirmed, "for now let's do it this way: you go

up tomorrow and take the radio with you. We'll keep in touch and if, when you get there, you see that you can establish Camp 3, I'll send Gogna, Barbacetto and Leviti up immediately so that they'll be there within three days to replace you without having to push themselves. Tell me if that's all right."

Messner answered straight away: "That's great, if we reach Camp 3 today, they can leave for Camp 1 today too."

At around 8.30., they started the climb from Camp 2 and at 11 a.m. told me they were near the rocks: they had about another 150 metres to go and thought they would get there soon. In fact, at 12.30., they confirmed that they had reached their destination and were waiting for the Sherpas who had lagged behind. Seeing this good progress, I made Barbacetto, Gogna and Leviti leave for Camp 1 with a Sherpa to relieve the first team as we had arranged.

At 6.30, I got in touch with Reinhold again, who warned me that they needed more rope because the porters had used it all up on the more difficult sections: the ones fixed by Gogna and Barbacetto on the 18th were all buried in snow. During this radio contact, Messner talked at length, expressing his admiration for how much Det had done preparing the route to Camp 3 and proposing, with his usual technical precision, his projected programme. He then called Camp 2 with a list of what he needed next day: titanium pitons, gas cartridges, ropes. Det took it down and responded in lively tones to his young friend's demands for food, which was running short up there.

"Well, now you're so used to living without eating," he radioed, "you can surely last a week!"

In the same radio transmission, when I spoke to Camp 2, where Alippi and Conti were, Det, all enthusiasm, told me: "Riccardo, I am really happy to have reached 7,000 metres, even though I am exhausted." During the 7 a.m. transmission on the morning of the 4th, I heard that the wind was so strong, not only at Camp 2 but also at 3, that they couldn't even get out of their tents. Later it dropped, and Ang Tsering and two other Sherpas carried food and 300 metres of rope to Camp 3, where Curnis and Messner worked that afternoon and the next to fix them and open the route to Camp 4.

From Base Camp on May 7, we saw Gogna and Barbacetto, who had taken over from Messner and Curnis, attacking the snow slope above Camp 3. They moved up to the end of the pyramid and, as the second climber veered left behind the corner, disappeared from sight. We found out later that Gogna and Barbacetto had fixed a lot of rope on the slope above Camp 3, reaching an altitude of 7,500 metres, 30 or so metres below the ridge. This was the highest altitude reached.

Leviti arrived at 3 that evening and stayed with Barbacetto, while Gogna, in turn, went to Camp 2. The first pair then pitched another tent a little more to the left and, following the advice that Messner radioed them from beside me, they tucked the tent as far as possible under the serac. In the 6.30 transmission, Barbacetto told me that small slides were continuously falling down the wall and ending up round the tent: in less than half an hour about 30 centimetres of snow had fallen. We agreed to call each other at 8 p.m. But when I turned on the radio in the main tent for the contact, I heard Gogna's voice from Camp 2 saying: "Riccardo, Camp 3 has disappeared!"

Those few words left us petrified. After the first moments of shock, I asked for news of the two climbers and heard with great relief that Leviti and Barbacetto were safe.

"There must be about 20 centimetres of snow, but there's no wind," continued Gogna.

"That's the problem," I answered. "If there had been a wind it would have taken the snow away bit by bit and there wouldn't have been a slide. We can only hope that they'll be able to dig themselves out and set up a bivouac good enough to protect them so they won't have too hard a time."

"This shouldn't have happened," Sandro added. "The only night that there should have been wind, there wasn't any."

We kept on talking while I tried to contact Camp 3 directly. "It's just bad luck, we've had bad luck from the beginning and it'll dog us to the end. How can we go on like this risking people's lives?" I said.

"I don't know what you guys think, but it looks pretty

black up here," answered Gogna. "And to think that if this hadn't happened, we could have gone on: we had high hopes. I'm very sorry, you know; it's your decision. I only wish we had the wings to succeed!"

Those lads were marvellous and deeply touching especially in the most difficult moments. They certainly deserved better luck.

Sandro then told me he intended to go up to Leviti and Barbacetto in case they needed anything; but I persuaded him — actually, I ordered him — not to move so as not to expose himself needlessly to danger. I advised him to wait for his companions at Camp 2, so that they could all come down together. Finally, I heard Barbacetto's voice, which was a great relief:

"Well, Riccardo, everything's going quite well, we're trying to dig the shovel out of the snow; don't worry about us because we're fine." And he told me everything that had happened.

The avalanche came down around 7.30. The men were squeezed against the wall of the serac while they were in the tent making something to eat, and they suddenly found themselves 'mouth to mouth' in a tiny space that continued to shrink. The cooker went out but the gas cylinder was still open and the gas went on escaping. They could not shut it off because they were stuck under the snow: they were in a small gas chamber. With great presence of mind, Leviti broke his glasses and, with a piece of lens, pierced the left side of the tent, where he presumed there would be less snow, and thus made a small opening from which they managed with great difficulty to escape. Fortunately for them, one of them had his crampons on, and the other had been sitting above him. With one glove between them (the others were still buried inside the bags) they dug themselves out, recovered the radio and a battery, and had contacted first Gogna and later, around 8.30, us. They had also managed to find the sleeping bags and could spend the night in a hole they had dug in the snow.

We kept in constant contact until we were sure they had recovered everything necessary to bivouac, and also to let them feel in some way our affection and presence. "Try to have as good a night as you can," I told them, adding whatever advice and support I could think to give them.

In the morning, as agreed, we established contact at six: the news was good. Fortunately the wind, contrary to its usual practice did not blow that night; otherwise it would have caused a real disaster.

"Collect what you can and make an inventory of what's left to see if it's worthwhile for us to come up and get it. Then come down as soon as you can, the minute the sun warms you up," I told them, and added that Gogna was waiting for them at Camp 2. Aldo spoke to me too, to put my mind at rest, with some splendidly jolly singing:

"I'm here sun-bathing," he told me, "and last night we did quite well: I sang some nice songs. . . . I even managed to sleep too. I don't know about Sereno but we're just fine." Then he added — and this gave me an accurate estimate of how the two boys had minimized their predicament — "but look, honestly, everything's wiped out here. You should see the tent poles: some of them make two 90-degree turns."

I thought of the importance of having placed the tent under the roof-like serac, as Messner had advised: otherwise they would have been swept away. I also considered the risk they ran when, since the gas cylinder was still releasing gas inside the tent, Barbacetto had opened the oxygen tank: with such a mixture, one spark would have been enough to cause a fatal explosion.

Meanwhile, we met at Base Camp to decide what to do after this new blow, which had eliminated the possibility of reaching the top because we no longer had enough time or tents. We eventually settled on a plan of reaching the ridge and then going down the Khumbu Glacier, thus making the first crossing of the great Nuptse-Lhotse rampart. We calculated the equipment we needed, tents, sleeping bags, foam pads, which we still had and could use, and then sent the Sherpas and the porters to Camp 1 with the materials and the necessary supplies. At Base Camp everyone, depending on experience, made his contribution, whether in arranging the cableway or reactivating the necessary camps: once again the spirit of co-operation was rekindled for the success of the new project. They were good lads, loyal and capable: each one did his best and I can truly say that I am proud to have led them.

However, the weather did not want to help us; in fact it opposed us, alternating between clear weather and heavy snowfall, just when we were most committed to the project. Thus on the 10th, Det, Conti and Lorenzi, who should have gone to Camp 3 to restore it, were stuck at Camp 2; there another 25 centimetres of fresh snow had fallen. I advised them to come down before another avalanche, so they returned to Base Camp during the evening. During the night it snowed uninterruptedly, and in the morning there were about 60 centimetres of fresh snow on the face. We had to give up.

On the 12th, after clearing briefly, the weather became unstable again. Next day Curnis and Det were to go and see if it were possible to get up to Camp 2 to recover the equipment. Meanwhile, the official Nepalese radio announced that two members of the Anglo-Nepalese Nuptse Expedition, both English, had not returned from the final assault on the 10th. We found out later that during the attempted rescue operation two other members were swept away by an avalanche*. We knew all four of the lost men, having met them at Dingpoche and during the preparatory phase of the project we had often stayed at each other's camps. They had also taken care of our Dr. Chierego and had been truly good friends to us. It had seemed that theirs was a softer expedition, on a normal route all the way up a ridge and not very difficult. For almost three years, since Messner's victory in 1972 on Manaslu's South Face, no Himalayan expedition, with the exception of those on normal routes, had been successful in reaching its objective, because of the prohibitive weather conditions. On top of this, there had been numerous painful losses of life.

On the morning of the 13th, the clouds thickened, but Det and Curnis left all the same for Camp 1. Around 2 p.m., it

* Gerry Owens and Richard Summerton died during an abortive summit bid and David Brister and Pasang Sherpa fell during the subsequent retreat. Sources: *Mountain 45* and *The Alpine Journal 1976.*

was already snowing and later Mario radioed me that higher up there were more than 10 centimetres of fresh snow, but that they had reached the old Camp 1 with a struggle. They came back that evening to Base Camp which was also covered with a thick blanket of snow, 25 centimetres deep. Piussi and Messner went to Namche to get a message to Colonel Ondgi to send us money to pay off the Sherpas and hire the porters for our return. Reinhold thus met his wife, who had come up to see him, and brought her up to Base Camp with her sister and a friend.

A sense of rebellion momentarily pervaded me, for it is human nature to try to overcome difficulties, to fight for success and to suffer from failure to reach the proposed goal. But I was far from being 'destroyed', as Messner later wrote in his book, *The Challenge.* That account of our expedition seems to me to rely on too much superficial psychology, and it makes me smile because my long experience in the mountains now enables me to evaluate both sad and happy events in a rather calmer manner. Nevertheless, this was my first mountaineering defeat, and the failure after all the sacrifices that we had made, was difficult to take. But I was moved by the brotherly greetings of my friend Chierego, the CAI representatives Emilio Orsini, Lodovico Gaetani and Giorgio Tiraboschi, who came all the way to Kathmandu to meet us in the name of the President, Giovanni Spagnolli. It showed a delicacy of feeling and a demonstration that what we had done, suffered, and decided was understood and appreciated by those who had entrusted me with this undertaking.

PART 6

Epilogue

CHAPTER TWENTY-ONE

The Mountains in Winter

In this book, I have rarely mentioned my activity in the mountains during the winter season: besides being a passionate climber, I am also a keen skier.

Since I was very young, I have been deeply involved in downhill skiing and have also practised jumping. The downhill and slalom had in the 1930's still not made their appearance. In the beginning, I remember, free-style downhill races were organized very quickly and simply: a starting point and a finishing point, the entire track being on virgin snow; it was, therefore, a genuinely 'off-piste' descent. Today skiing is a very widespread sport, not only for pleasure, but also for competition; but its origins, which are said to be extremely ancient, derived from the necessity of moving easily on snow-covered surfaces. The sport was therefore born as a means of transport when skis supplanted the primitive snow shoes.

Until around 1935, ski lifts didn't exist, which favoured the development of cross-country skiing, a wonderfully exhilarating way of venturing into the mountains and exploring them in the winter and spring, of enjoying their beauty, of savouring the immense pleasure of a descent on virgin snow after the healthy struggle of the climb.

I remember my first indispensable set of sealskins (made from the actual skin of the animal, whereas today they are made of synthetic fibre) and my first unforgettable trips in those years now so long past.

Progress, and the ever-increasing number of winter sports centres, with their various ways of getting up hill, favoured the development of mass skiing intended mainly for fun, and almost caused the abandonment of cross-country skiing. In fact, in the years following the Second World War, this type of skiing became the preserve of only the *appassionati*, and was considered by the normal frequenters of the pistes as an exercise in nostalgia. Nevertheless, the excessive development of downhill skiing on the piste, and the long queues on the slopes, are bringing the really passionate skiers back to ski-mountaineering, a perfect combination of two disciplines that allows one to get close to the mountains even in winter in less spoiled settings.

During winter and spring, I always go skiing and never climb intensively. For me winter faces have characteristics far different from those of summer. The north faces, even if very steep, are always colder and covered with snow in the winter season, because the sun never touches them, and the difficulties increase, and change, while on the south faces, except for the colder weather and the reduced hours of daylight, almost the same conditions as in the summer are found because of their exposure to the sun. Although the sun is not so hot, it melts the snow so that it easily falls off the vertical walls: and at times they are in better condition than in the summer because the danger of loose holds and stonefall is less. On moderately difficult routes, given their lesser angle, the snow remains much longer; during the day it partly melts, wets the wall, and in the cold of the night forms verglas, which makes ascents more difficult and, at times, impossible.

I do not want to detract from the merit and value of winter ascents made by others, but I can only say that for my own satisfaction, during the winter, I prefer skiing activities, which combine with alpine training and allow me to go on ski-tours across all the classic routes of the Alps and Pre-Alps. This sport demands serious preparation, a good understanding of mountains, and informed judgement of the snow cover on which you move, in terms of thickness and layering. In fact, these vary according to geological formation, exposure, time of day, the particular season, and the altitude. These important factors must be kept in mind to avoid the risk of being swept away by avalanche.

While on the subject, I remember a trip made in the winter of 1960/61 with my friend Pierino Zanga across the easy traverse from Piani di Artavaggio to Paini di Bobbio. Having reached the Bocchetta dei Mughi on solid and stable snow, we started to go down the opposite side towards Bobbio. I was ahead of my friend and had done only two turns on my skis when I suddenly felt I was being dragged backwards. At first, I didn't understand what was happening, but then I found myself rolling in a mass of snow that I had detached, and getting immersed in it.

Fortunately, I remembered that by 'swimming in the snow' you can stay afloat and rise to the surface. I did this and can confirm that it is actually true, even if it takes considerable effort, so much so that if I stopped the swimming movement for one moment I was immediately sucked under again. After trying again two or three times, I was literally thrown into space: luckily I landed on my feet, with only my head out of the mass of snow. With rapid movements, I wriggled my body back and forth to make room in my hole, knowing that if I were to stop the snow would solidify and imprison me.

I tried to get out of the trap, but could only free the leg from which my ski had fallen off; the other was bound by the safety strap on the ski. With one hand, thanks to the space I had made previously, I managed to unhook it, climb straight out from that uncomfortable position and call out to my friend, who thought me swept away by the avalanche. With only one ski and a tremendous effort, I reached the Piani di Bobbio.

This adventure, which fortunately ended happily, helped me acquire part of that necessary experience on which I have relied for many years, and on which I still continue to rely, in the magnificent sport of ski-mountaineering.

CHAPTER TWENTY-TWO

Mountain Rescue

A live body to be saved, a dead one to recover: this tragic alternative lies behind the all-too-frequent rescue calls in the mountains that surround Lecco. From the moment of the call, every succeeding second becomes more precious. You scramble up trails and climb rocks, competing with time, often struggling against dreadful weather conditions, to carry out a self-imposed task, a spontaneous response to our human consciences.

It would be practically impossible for me to remember and enumerate all the mountain rescues in which I have participated. I will only touch on those which have had the greatest impact on my memory; of many others, I only remember that moving moment when a wounded person is reached on a wall, or the cruel encounter with death in the rigidity of a poor tortured body.

My first mountain rescue dates back to 1928 on the Fasana Wall, after the first winter attempt which ended tragically with the death of Cattaneo and Veronelli. I don't remember who had called the team which came from Cervinia to recover their bodies that, for some days, had been lying on that wall. At the time, besides being very young, I was completely inexperienced, and for me and my companions it was humiliating to see a team arrive from another area. But what hit me most was the fact that instead of the bodies being lowered to the valley, they were dropped. I remember the horror we felt in seeing this done with a coldness that seemed cruel to me. True, they were dealing with dead bodies, but this method revolted us: it wasn't part of our mentality, and it never became part of our behaviour as a mountain rescue team.

In the autumn of 1943, during the Second World War, a group of young climbers, one of whom was a woman, got trapped by a sudden change in the weather on the Segantini

Ridge of our Grignetta. The leader of the group, the most experienced, was hurt in a fall; the others completely lost their bearings because of the snow which fell constantly, levelling and smoothing everything out. Lost, and in those conditions, they spent an evil night out.

The following day, I was with my friends, (those few who were left: some were in the war, and others in the mountains as fugitives) heading towards the 'direttissima' of the Grignetta when we met a boy, one of the youngest of the group, coming down alone. We asked him for news of his group: he answered that some were only a short way away and two others were still on the Segantini Ridge because one of them was hurt. We helped him and fed him; then we advised him to go down to the valley immediately. With considerable difficulty, because we were hindered by the excessive amount of fresh snow, we went on to look for the unfortunate ones. We met the first group, two men and a girl, in the couloir before that of the Val Tesa. We did our best to revive and comfort them; they were wet through and numb. The two men especially seemed to have been through a lot, while the woman looked in better condition. I took off my sweater to cover her, for she was completely soaked, and we wrapped the three of them up in what we had with us. I then entrusted my friends with getting them down to the valley, while I went up to help Dell'Oro (Boga) and Gigi Vitali who had gone ahead to rescue the other two on the ridge.

So much snow had fallen that I could not see any traces of my companions who had gone ahead of me. I climbed the Val Tesa couloir as far as the bottom of Guglia Angelina: I called again and again but there was no reply. In fact, they couldn't hear me because the wind was so strong it blew away my voice. And all the time the snow continued to fall. However, I didn't give up, and finally succeeded in communicating with them. They had heard the two on the ridge and talked to them, but they couldn't go any further because of the savage weather and the ever-increasing danger of avalanches. I advised them to come down. By now my two friends could no longer hear any calls from above and decided to rappel down, convinced that those two were dead.

With difficulty we managed to find our companions, who unfortunately had not moved from the point where I had left them: to my horror and dismay, I realized the two men were dead, while the girl was still breathing, though she was very ill and in a coma. We did everything possible to carry her, in conditions made desperately precarious not only by the mountain but also by our rather inadequate equipment. We started the descent, but after covering about a 100 metres the poor soul succumbed. We tied her body to the rocks and hurried down to get ourselves out of danger. Many of the rescue team were complaining of the initial stages of frost-bite.

At the Piani dei Resinelli, we went to the SEL (Società Escursionisti Lecchesi) Hut to dry out and warm up a little. After a few hours, towards sunset, an acquaintance of ours came to call us because he had heard a cry for help coming from the 'direttissima'. We were stupified. We could barely believe it because we had just come down from that same face. I dressed as best I could in the driest clothes I had, threw on a pair of clogs and hurried to the Chiesetta to see if it were true. I too heard the calls.

I borrowed a pair of boots and socks from my friend Cuera, and went up towards the 'direttissima', calling out every once in a while to keep my bearings in the poor visibility, and also to give moral support to the unfortunate person up there. Trying to locate him, I realized he was no longer on the track to the 'direttissima', but had gone down to the tree line. While I was still some distance away he yelled: "Cassin, Cassin, save me and I'll give you five hundred lire" (a very large sum in those days). I smiled inwardly, despite everything, and assured him I would certainly take him to safety.

Following his voice, I reached him, fed him, and told him to get going, but then I realized that his nerves had relaxed because of the knowledge of being safe, and played him a dirty trick. He could no longer stand on his feet, nor walk, and complained that his whole body hurt. I was forced to carry him on my shoulders. He carried on in an agitated fashion, yelling and pleading that he wanted to stay there to die. Having reached the altitude of the cave above the Resinelli, I met a peasant who helped me carry him all the way to the Cuera Hut, where we massaged him and gave him what he needed. As to the promised payment, apart from the fact that I certainly would not have accepted it, it was not offered nor mentioned again. In fact, on occasions when I happen to meet him, he tries to avoid me and pretends not to recognise me.

The following day, in better weather, we recovered the three bodies, and saw to the one left on the ridge a few days later.

In the summer of 1949, while I was working in my shop busy with a French group whom I knew and who had come to buy some equipment, I had a 'phone call from the Piani dei Resinelli: "Cassin," it said, "there's a man on the Mushroom (Fungo), hanging under the slabs, you can even see him from here, and his mate has soloed down for help." I called my friends, and two or three of the Frenchmen offered to come with us too. We left immediately for the Resinelli and reached the bottom of the Fungo in the dark. With Dell'Oro and two Frenchmen, I climbed up to the beginning of the traverse of the Fungo: we had to hold our torches in our mouths while we climbed (head torches didn't exist in those days).

I reached the piton that was holding the poor fellow, who was still talking sense, and lowered him a rope with a karabiner so that he could clip in and I could bring him up. Unfortunately, he couldn't manage to unclip the karabiner, so I had to reverse down the slab and send up Dell'Oro, who was lighter, making him go down the rope and clip in the poor lad.

With tremendous effort, we recovered him and took him to the saddle of the Fungo. We made him swallow a drink with stimulants in it to revive him, but he passed out. His condition looked very serious, though his respiration and heartbeat were normal. Helped by my companions who belayed me, I carried him on my shoulders from that point to the fork between Lancia and Torre. We lowered him down to the bottom, put him in a stretcher and wrapped him in blankets, but a furious storm and the darkness prevented us from taking him to the valley. In the morning we succeeded, and saw with satisfaction that, thanks to the medicine and care, our invalid was fine and was certainly more rested than we. Our team remembers this rescue in particular because, for many years after on the anniversary of the rescue, the boy's father would send us money for a happy drinking session.

The Lecco CAI Rescue Team, which was responsible for rescue work for a long time, had no help at that time. Only later did the city administration give us a grant, which allowed us to cover at least part of our expenses: the rest we still have to find ourselves, as well as the loss of working days.

CHAPTER TWENTY-THREE

Past and Present

Thoughts and considerations crowd my mind at the closing point in this account of my 50-year dialogue with the mountains. It has been a fast race across time, following the most obvious phases in the development of climbing.

The use of equipment and the adoption of systems to facilitate climbing really began in this century; nevertheless, even the pioneers of alpinism were not afraid to resort to artificial means to succeed in their intent. Remember the ladders de Saussure brought to climb Mt. Blanc, and those Tyndall took to the Matterhorn, and again the steel nails and grappling hook used on the Matterhorn by Carrel and Whymper. These were undoubtedly primitive means, but they reveal the nature of the climber: to use intelligence and whatever is available to reach the proposed goal.

The progress of artificial climbing encountered tenacious resistance, in the true sense, only in the person of Paul Preuss: artificial methods were not accepted by this great alpinist even for protection, but unfortunately, he fell to his death at the early age of 27.

I personally started by free climbing, at first using pitons only for protection, but soon for aid too; only with the use of double ropes and etriers was I able to do routes on the Grignetta and in the Alps on terrain where, by free climbing, ascents would not have been possible. In those days long ago, many applauded me but many more censored me, calling me and my companions 'ironmongers'.

Some say that climbing is finished: the same thing was said in the first ten years of the century, when pitons, pendulums and double-rope descents came on the scene. The great conquests that followed, and still continue, show how far off the track these prophets were. The system of artificial climb-

*Preuss fell to his death while attempting to solo the North Face of the Manndlkogel in the Gosaukamm in 1913. *Publisher's note*

ing from Comici's time to the present has been completely refined: progress and innovations continue, to the climber's advantage. For example, I can complete climbs in less time and with less effort than many years ago, and reach the top still fresh despite my age, helped in part by experience, but more perhaps by modern techniques and equipment. Naturally, the unjustified use of pitons certainly doesn't reflect well on someone who climbs a route that way.

I must also say that, without any shadow of a doubt, climbing with expansion bolts in my opinion can never be that which intrigues the real climber — the true solution to a particular piece of rock. In using them, we are no longer dealing with the secret of finding a tiny weakness, perhaps the only one that may constitute the key for a new route. On the other hand, the possibility of climbing new and important routes in the Alps seemed for a time almost eliminated, and the little that remained was of such a nature as to force climbers to use other methods, and resort increasingly to extreme technical manoeuvres. However, this does not in itself constitute the end of climbing; it is its modern mode created by necessity.

Progress comes about in all fields and in all sports: I do not see why there cannot also be change in this discipline. Every climber has the right to go to the mountains however he chooses, and so in my opinion present-day climbing is widely democratic: but let it be logical, let it not become reduced to mere brief exploits, let the underlying motive in the fight against extreme difficulty always be the search for healthy pleasure and spiritual elevation which that strenuous and often dangerous battle against rock and ice brings, whether or not the final outcome is success. Then climbing should give satisfaction and its just rewards, though never medals or prizes, for the true climber abhors them.

Let us go into the mountains, then, with a sense of continuity, and a lack of presumption! The exceptional feats seem at times to have removed from climbing that fascination with the impossible that has always been the secret drive behind any great conquest. But these cannot make mountains ever cease to be a tremendously uplifting source of aesthetic and ethical sensations that spiritually enrich us.

In this spirit, therefore, I feel that my dialogue with mountains is not over.

First Ascents by Riccardo Cassin

1931		
Guglia Angelina, East Face	Grigna	Mary Varale
Sigaro Dones, North Edge	Grigna	Giovanni Riva
Corna di Medale, S.S.E. Face	Grigna	Mario Dell'Oro
Torrione Palma, S.W. Face	Grigna	Riccardo Redaelli
1932		
Sasso dei Carbonari, S.E. Face	Grigna	Mario Dell'Oro
Pizzo della Pieve, N.E. Face	Grigna	Mario Dell'Oro, Giuseppe Comi
Pizzo d'Eghen, West Face	Grigna	Carlo Corti
Guglia Angelina, West Face	Grigna	Mario Dell'Oro, Mary Varale
1933		
Torrione Magnaghi, S.E. Face	Grigna	Cariboni Rizieri
Corno del Nibbio, East Face	Grigna	Antonio Piloni, Augusto Corti
Torre Costanza, South Face	Grigna	Antonio Piloni, Domenico Lazzeri
Sasso Cavallo, South Face	Grigna	Augusto Corti
Torre Costanza, East Face	Grigna	Mario Dell'Oro, Mary Varale
Corno del Nibbio, East Face	Grigna	Mario Dell'Oro, Panzeri
1934		
Pizzo della Pieve, N.E. Face	Grigna	Augusto Corti
C. della Bagozza, North Spur	Camino Gr.	Aldo Frattini, Rodolfo Varallo
Cima Piccolissima, North Face	Dolomites	Gigi Vitali, Luigi Pozzi
1935		
Mt. Civetta, N. Face (variation)	Dolomites	Mario Dell'Oro
Torre Trieste, S.E. Face	Dolomites	Vittorio Ratti
Cima Ovest, North Face	Dolomites	Vittorio Ratti
1937		
Piz Badile, N.E. Face	Bregaglia	Vittorio Ratti, Gino Esposito (also Molteni and Valsecchi)
1938		
Grandes Jorasses, Walker Spur	W. Alps	Gino Esposito, Ugo Tizzoni
1939		
Golem, East Face	Concarena	Pierino Cattaneo
1940		
Aig. du Leschaux, North Face	W. Alps	Ugo Tizzoni

1947		
Sorelle di Sorapis, N.W. Face	Dolomites	Felice Butti
Torre del Diavolo, S.E. Face	Dolomites	Carlo Mauri
1961		
Mt. McKinley, South Face	Alaska	Gigi Alippi, Romano Perego Jack Canali, Annibale Zucchi, Luigi Airoldi
1969		
Jirishanca, West Face	Andes	Mimmo Lanzetta, Sandro Liati Casimiro Ferrari Giuseppe Lafranconi, Annibale Zucchi

Other Expeditions led by Riccardo Cassin

1957 Gasherbrum IV (Successful — summit reached by Walter Bonatti and Carlo Mauri)

1975 Lhotse South Face (Unsuccessful — highest point reached was 7500 metres)

Bibliography

Some relevant books and articles in English:

American Alpine Journal 1963, 1970, 1976
Bonatti, Walter, *On the Heights* Diadem Books, London 1979
Desio, Prof. Ardito, *The Ascent of K2* Paul Elek, London 1955
Gervasutti, Giusto, *Gervasutti's Climbs* Diadem Books, London 1978
The Mountaineers, Seattle 1979
Harrer, Heinrich, *The White Spider* Granada Publishing, London 1976
Heckmair, Anderl, *My Life as a Mountaineer* Victor Gollancz, London 1975
Mountain 25 *Grandes Jorasses Commentary* by Alessandro Gogna
Mountain 28 *Piz Badile Commentary* by Colin Taylor
Mountain 32 *Interview with Riccardo Cassin*
Mountain 45 *The World's Highest Mountains: Nuptse* by G. O. Dyhrenfurth
Mountain 49 *The World's Highest Mountains: Gasherbrum IV* by G. O. Dyhrenfurth
Mountain 66 *The World's Highest Mountains: Lhotse* by G. O. and N. Dyhrenfurth
Mountain 70 *The World's Highest Mountains: K2* by G. O. and N. Dyhrenfurth
Noyce, Wilfrid, and McMorrin, Ian, *World Atlas of Mountaineering* Thomas Nelson, London 1969
Jones, Chris, *Climbing in North America* University of California Press, 1976, Diadem Books, London 1979
Messner, Reinhold, *The Challenge* Kaye and Ward, London 1977; Oxford University Press, New York 1977
Mariani, Fosco, *Karakoram: The Ascent of Gasherbrum IV* Hutchinson, London 1961; The Viking Press, New York 1964
Rebuffat, Gaston, *Starlight and Storm* Kaye and Ward, London 1969; Oxford University Press, New York, 1969
Scott, Doug, *Big Wall Climbing* Kaye and Ward, London 1974; Oxford University Press, New York, 1974
Pause, Walter, and Winkler, Wolf Jürgen, *Extreme Alpine Rock* Granada, 1979

Index